MARKETING CHRONICLES

MARKETING CHRONICLES

A Compendium of Global and Local Marketing Insights from the Pre-Smartphone and Post-Smartphone Eras

NIMISH V. DWIVEDI

Notion Press

Old No. 38, New No. 6
McNichols Road, Chetpet
Chennai - 600 031

First Published by Notion Press 2017
Copyright © Nimish V. Dwivedi 2017
All Rights Reserved.

ISBN 978-1-947949-15-7

This book has been published with all reasonable efforts taken to make the material error-free after the consent of the author. No part of this book shall be used, reproduced in any manner whatsoever without written permission from the author, except in the case of brief quotations embodied in critical articles and reviews.

The Author of this book is solely responsible and liable for its content including but not limited to the views, representations, descriptions, statements, information, opinions and references ["Content"]. The Content of this book shall not constitute or be construed or deemed to reflect the opinion or expression of the Publisher or Editor. Neither the Publisher nor Editor endorse or approve the Content of this book or guarantee the reliability, accuracy or completeness of the Content published herein and do not make any representations or warranties of any kind, express or implied, including but not limited to the implied warranties of merchantability, fitness for a particular purpose. The Publisher and Editor shall not be liable whatsoever for any errors, omissions, whether such errors or omissions result from negligence, accident, or any other cause or claims for loss or damages of any kind, including without limitation, indirect or consequential loss or damage arising out of use, inability to use, or about the reliability, accuracy or sufficiency of the information contained in this book.

CONTENTS

Acknowledgements — ix
About the Author — xi
Book Reviews — xiii

PART 1: PRE-SMARTPHONE ERA INSIGHTS

Chapter 1: Redefining Rail and Road Travel through Convenience, Comfort and Affordability (1998) — 3

Chapter 2: The Greatest Enemy of the Marketing Fraternity in the Last Ten Years (1999) — 7

Chapter 3: The Concept of Category Catalysts (2002) — 11

Chapter 4: An Unconventional Source of Learnings on Making a Relaunch Work (2002) — 15

Chapter 5: The Scourge of Marginal Marketing (2004) — 18

Chapter 6: The 360-degree Spin (2006) — 22

PART 2: POST SMARTPHONE ERA INSIGHTS

Chapter 7: The Emerging and Highly Relevant Concept of 'Customer Interaction Models' (2009) — 29

Chapter 8: Beat the Blues! Upbeat Business Models during an Overall Downturn (2009) — 34

Contents

Chapter 9: The Growing Power of "Brand Buzz" And "Brand Chatter" (2009) — 39

Chapter 10: Making Sense of the Financial Crisis and Linked Fundamental Actions (2009) — 43

Chapter 11: The Greatest Generation? (2009) — 47

Chapter 12: Mallifying Them with Choice (2009) — 50

Chapter 13: The Afterlife of Categories and Brands (2009) — 55

Chapter 14: Metropolis Metrics Like Marketing Metrics — 60

Chapter 15: Four McIdlies and a Kentucky Baked Vada, Please (2010) — 65

Chapter 16: Packaging – the Fifth P of Marketing (2010) — 68

Chapter 17: Rethinking Your Sports Marketing Move (Basis the 2010 FIFA World Cup South Africa) — 72

Chapter 18: India's Inadvertent Exports (2010) — 76

Chapter 19: Social Networking – Connect Where It Matters (2010) — 80

Chapter 20: The All-In-One Brand Proposition (2010) — 82

Chapter 21: Caring for India's Ignored Generation (2010) — 85

Chapter 22: How India Can Help NRIs Invest (2011) — 88

Chapter 23: The Building Blocks of Outdoor Media (2011) — 91

Chapter 24: Beyond Visual Appeal – The Tougher Elements of an Ad Campaign (2016) — 93

Chapter 25: Factoring in First Impressions to Create Brand Loyalty (2016) — 96

Chapter 26: The Left-Out Segment (2016) — 99

Chapter 27: Adding the "Viability" Perspective to the Business of Financial Inclusion — 103

Chapter 28: Throwback to Turntables – How Nostalgia Can Work Wonders for the Marketing Mix (2016) — 106

Chapter 29: Road Safety Gear – an Untapped Route (2016) — 109

Chapter 30: From Start-Up to Scaled-Up (2016) — 114

Contents

Chapter 31:	The Age of 'Flash Phenomena'– Why Is It That Some Things Become a Global Rage and Then Just Disappear? (2016)	118
Chapter 32:	Slowing Down, Gaining Rapidly (2016)	121
Chapter 33:	CMOs Need to Go Take a Walk (2017)	124
Chapter 34:	The Rise of D-Babas! (2017)	127
Chapter 35:	The Need for Senior Citizens' Banks (2017)	130
Chapter 36:	From Cost-First to Customer-First (2017)	132
Chapter 37:	Rebooting the "Curry" Category (2017)	134

ACKNOWLEDGEMENTS

For my dear mom who is always blessing me from above.
For dad, for always standing by me.

Thanks To

Tarun Gupta, Professor of marketing at JBIMS, for inculcating me into the world of marketing – Bharat Puri and PG Ponnapa, for the learnings at Asian Paints.

Sandeep Chakrabarti, for the wonderful inputs at Standard Chartered.

Ajay Makhija at Citibank.

Special Thanks To
Farhad Irani for always believing in me.

Special Thanks Also

To the teams at Business Line, Business Standard, Brand Equity, Campaign, AWSJ, and the many other publications which have published all of the work that forms this compendium.

ABOUT THE AUTHOR

Nimish V. Dwivedi is a consumer marketing and financial services professional who has observed the changing and emerging landscape of marketing through living and working in Japan, Hong Kong, Singapore, UAE and Vietnam, besides always observing India outside in.

Having graduated with a marketing major from one of India's top business schools – Jamnalal Bajaj Institute of Management Studies, Nimish has had the privilege of working with and learning from some of the best marketing professionals in the industry. Starting his career fresh out of campus as an executive trainee at Asian Paints, Nimish has worked in senior leadership roles at Citibank, Standard Chartered, Paypal, Mashreq Bank and is currently the Business Director Cards and Payments at VP Bank-FE Credit, based in Vietnam.

Nimish has been able to practice and execute his marketing perspectives besides being a keen observer and an enthusiastic chronicler of the emerging marketing landscape, specifically in India besides in various other parts of the world.

BOOK REVIEWS

"A lucid, insightful and at times provocative look at brands and marketing over the years. Simple, well written and immensely readable, this is a must read for all observers, students and practitioners of marketing."

– *Bharat Puri*
Managing Director, Pidilite Industries.
Former President, Global Chocolate, Gum and Candy, Mondelez International; Former Senior VP, Global Chocolate, Kraft; Former Regional Commercial Director Asia Pacific, Cadbury Schweppes; Former MD, Cadbury South Asia.

"Nimish was always a diligent and thoughtful student in my Strategic Marketing class at Jamnalal Bajaj. Am delighted that he has chosen to share contemporary insights and perspectives on marketing from his two decade long career. Am sure this will be relevant for both practitioners and students of marketing and business."

– *Tarun Gupta*
Faculty at Jamnalal Bajaj, Consultant & Marketing Veteran.

Book Reviews

"Evolving Humans and Evolving Brands.

Thought provoking reading giving us insights about the future of brands."

– *Ajay Miglani*
Doon School, IIM Calcutta.

Former Marketing Director, Visa International
Founder of many successful entrepreneurial ventures:
Group Kankei/ND Commerce/Radii Rewards/Tiger Pug
Lived in India, Singapore, USA and China.

"Very few books capture the "romance" of marketing like this one. A must read for passionate Marketers and Brand Builders.

Overall, Nimish has always had a fresh take on varied consumer marketing topics. He brings in a rich and well rounded perspective. I haven't met a bigger romantic of consumer marketing as yet."

– *K. Venkatramani*
CEO, Heritage Brands Division, Arvind Fashions Ltd.

Held several leadership positions across Unilever, Levi Strauss, Bharti Walmart and Arvind Brands.

"About the Book: This book is a fascinating attempt by a uniquely perceptive and remarkable marketing professional to provide freedom to the art of classical marketing and let it innovate and evolve like the proverbial Mozart's symphony, using his remarkable repertoire of global marketing stories.

About Nimish: Nimish is what I call a "provocative" marketing professional – one who is never satisfied with the obvious, is always searching for the "camouflaged" insight, and keeps pushing his superiors, his organization and his industry to not only accept and overcome, but create new challenges."

– Ajay Makhija

Former Board member at Samba Capital and
Former Group Head, Global Consumer Banking at
Samba Financial Group, Riyadh, Saudi Arabia;
Former Country Business Manager, Consumer Bank, Egypt
Former Head of Liabilities Product, Asia Pacific.

PART 1

PRE-SMARTPHONE ERA INSIGHTS

CHAPTER 1

REDEFINING RAIL AND ROAD TRAVEL THROUGH CONVENIENCE, COMFORT AND AFFORDABILITY (1998)

The power of focusing on the segment travelling by road and rail in India

"It takes a lot to get there and more effort when you arrive, but unless you can make the journey you are confined to one valley of thought all your life," muses Robert Pirsig in his cult book *Zen and the Art of Motorcycle Maintenance*.

Since the beginning of time, man has been a travelling animal. First, in search of food and shelter, then in pursuit of adventure. Man's wanderlust is a manifestation of his optimism, of his belief that there is another side to the fence and that the grass is greener there. Man travels because of an inherent sense of opportunity.

Earlier, travelling meant sailing the seven seas. Now, it means flying over them. Mention business travel today, and it conjures an image of a pinstripe-suited, starched-collared yuppie armed with a cellphone in one hand and a laptop in the other – someone who spends half his life strapped to airplane seats, and zips in and out of boardrooms and five-star hotels with equal elan.

For this individual, the world is a global village and India is a mere bylane. A host of companies are trying to become the preferred brand for this profile of customers. Marketers of laptops, electric shavers, upmarket luggage, cellphones and wrinkle free shirts vie for space in the crowded recesses of this customer's mind.

However, the categories that have been really active to attract and retain this archetypal business traveller are hotels and airlines. Many airlines have launched frequent flyer programmes to become the preferred choice of these customers. Such companies also understand that though these travellers' expenses are borne by their organisations, it is the power of individual rewards that will ensure repeat business. What could be more pleasurable than accumulating flying return points on official travel and redeeming them for a free trip to a holiday destination?

Realising that the proposition becomes far more exciting if an individual can be rewarded with air miles, many airlines are pursuing the possibility of issuing a co-branded credit card. In this case, a credit card company and a partner combine their strengths to create a set of benefits for their customers, which neither of them can offer on a standalone basis. Where airlines are partners, the customer is awarded mileage points for all his spends on the card. This dramatically increases the opportunities to accumulate mileage points. The customer gets a never-before benefit, the card company gets more cards and higher spends, and the airline gets a loyal customer. It's a win-win for all concerned.

In the future, as is the trend in developed markets, the concept of co-branding is likely to move further with the advent of multi-branded credit cards. These are developed to fulfil the needs of a specific segment, of which the business traveller is just one. Imagine if a hotel chain, an airline, a cellular phone company, and a business information provider were to partner with a bank and issue a multi-branded credit card. The combined strength could reward the individual in a way that no two partners could ever do. And even the customer would be able to redeem his reward points not just for air miles but for a range of products offered by the multi-brand partners including room nights, cellular airtime and even business information subscriptions.

Where there is a lot of marketing activity aimed at attracting and retaining the upper-end business traveller, organisations need to ask themselves who really is a business traveller in the Indian context? If we restrict our definition to the power-dressing, strolley-toting minute manager, then we are blinding ourselves to a tremendous opportunity.

The millions of salesmen who travel to remote villages using the most uncomfortable means of transport are also business travellers. So are the traders and entrepreneurs travelling to grow their own businesses, enduring everything from dangerously-driven buses to crowded matador vans. Thousands of individuals who sit huddled in crowded trains are unable to sleep because they need to keep an eye on their luggage. These are the real business travellers in India – they are a segment for which obtaining a railway reservation is a gargantuan task, for whom basic comforts and conveniences do not even figure in the set of customer expectations. It is this segment which presents a tremendous marketing opportunity in the true sense.

Though this traveller may be lacking in glamour, within this large chunk, there is a sizeable set of customers who seek basic benefits, and importantly, have the ability and the willingness to pay for them. Today, there are very few options for such a traveller. Put yourself in their shoes for a minute; imagine you are taking a long business journey by road. What would be foremost on your mind? "How do I go about locating a clean and reasonably priced hotel?" Given the lack of published information, you would have to take advice from someone who has travelled that route before. "Where do I eat?" Again, your best bet would be to stop by at restaurants that seem to be doing brisk business. For this kind of business traveller, travel is an unorganised and unpleasurable experience. The key for marketing organisations lies in translating these gaps into opportunity.

It makes great sense, for example, to build a chain of restaurants along highways that offer quality food in a clean environment. Just as McDonald's stands for value cuisine, these restaurants can be trusted by all businessmen braving Indian roads in any part of the country.

Similarly, there is a colossal opportunity in transforming petrol pumps into "convenience points" along the highway, by equipping them with communication facilities, washrooms and stores that stock basic groceries, medicines, beverages and take-aways.

While co-branded cards with airlines have been a global success story, imagine the success story that could happen if the Indian Railways were to issue a co-branded credit card targeted at business travellers. This credit card could provide instant reservation in specially created business coaches. This cardholder could be offered a choice of meals aboard the train, which he could pay for with his credit card. They could also make calls and send faxes from the train, all billed to their cards. They could relax in the especially designated business waiting rooms if this train is delayed and withdraw cash from the ATMs located at the station. The card would also have the benefit of medical help at the stations and come with lost baggage insurance. The possibilities are endless. And best of all, these facilities could be provided at a cost which could still be more economical than the price of an air ticket.

With demand exceeding supply on most railway routes, the biggest question is "Why should the Railways do it?" The famous B-school case study on the US railroads suggests that these railroads declined because they never realised that they are in the transportation business and not just in the railroad business. Indian railways also must realise that to be more competitive they need to focus on making rail travel a far more convenient and comfortable experience, without losing their key attribute of affordability.

Similarly, Indian companies have to go beyond the image of the business traveller that advertising and blinkered perceptions have created, and realise that the real opportunity lies not just in selling hi-tech gadgets to customers but in redefining the business travel experience for a new generation of Indians.

CHAPTER 2

THE GREATEST ENEMY OF THE MARKETING FRATERNITY IN THE LAST TEN YEARS (1999)

With the new millennium just months away, media has been devoting plenty of newsprint to the men of the century, the newsmakers of the decade and the success and failures of an era that is rapidly passing into history books. Amidst all this, has anyone wondered who has been the greatest enemy of the marketing fraternity in the last ten years? The economic slowdown perhaps. Fickle customer loyalties maybe? The hands-down or rather fingers-down winner, however, is likely to be that most humble symbol of customer choice – the remote control.

The remote control, partnered by channel-explosion, has swung the balance of power entirely in favour of the viewers and their restless fingers. The result is a laser beam-empowered generation which cunningly sidesteps even the most powerful marketing messages with the flip of a button. And the marketers' response? Panic! Most marketers have invested millions in a range of devices and tracking mechanisms like PeopleMeter that try to gauge the fickleness of this generation of 'artful dodgers.' Some marketers, however, are fighting back. Their arsenal ranges from the run-of-the mill (sponsored programmes, entertaining ads, longer ads, imported ads with lots of blondes) to the innovative (contests linked to ads that promise big prizes in return for the viewer's concentration).

However, there does exist one attention-grabbing strategy that can combat the might of the remote control, and not many marketers have caught on to it yet. Let me give you an example: The Nokia Communicator is a product that combines the features of a cellular handset and a computer. It is by all means a complex product that would require massive investments in media for just elucidating the product concept, not to mention the media wastage, courtesy the remote control.

But rather than make a commercial to sell the Communicator, Nokia chose to give its product a starring role in a movie! In *The Saint*, a movie featuring Val Kilmer as a jet-setting master of disguises, the Communicator is his constant companion. While millions of viewers follow Kilmer's exploits with bated breath, they also get exposed to the brand and its benefits. The features register easily in the viewer's mind not because they are explained in technical terms but because the lead player actually uses all these features as an integral part of the movie's plot. I'll go one step further. Nokia's ploy is effective not so much because Kilmer uses this little gadget so prominently, but because the Communicator is a character by itself in the movie!

With this neat stroke, Nokia has transformed the concept of product placement. Till now, product placement meant a blinking neon flashing a brand name in the background while the actors did their bit on screen. But here, the product has an actual role to play in the movie. The concept of product placement has been advanced and made more meaningful – it can now be called 'Product Characterisation.'

Till now, product characterisation has been restricted to a handful of movies on the big screen. However, it is in the realm of 40-channel satellite television that the concept will truly come into its own. Product characterisation can be a powerful ally of marketers in the battle against the remote control. While watching a serial on television, viewers are involved with the characters and the storyline, and an advertising break between their favourite serial is nothing but an excuse to flip channels. But the message of a brand that is actually a part of the serial itself is bound to register and stands a very good chance of being remembered.

Let's take the example of one of India's most popular serials *Wagle Ki Duniya*. By definition, the serial's protagonists are value seekers who do not spend a single paise without thinking twice. What if the serial has an additional character: the family's modest but still favourite mode of transportation, their Bajaj scooter. Mr. Wagle could be shown experiencing the various attributes of this brand like reliability, sturdiness and fuel efficiency. The audience would get the message while soaking in their weekly dose of entertainment. And the impact of Mr. Wagle's kids humming '*Hamara Bajaj*' in an episode would have the impact of many 60-second-spots.

Or, imagine for example, if Bru coffee were to make an appearance in an episode of *Malgudi Days* where a crusty, old South Indian *mami* announces that she wants her morning Bru on the double, and no filter coffee for her, thank you!

Today, audiences can choose from a vast range of television serials involving a host of characters, each with their own style and traits. These are sure-shot product characterisation opportunities for many brands whose images are synchronised with these characters. Yes, this will certainly entail working in close conjunction with the makers of these serials. The brand has to be presented in these serials as a vibrant and communicating character. It goes without saying that characterisation has to be done in a manner that emphasises the core values of the brand.

Intelligent marketers will, no doubt, be able to turn product characterisation into a strategic marketing weapon. For those who are able to successfully bridge the gap between art and persuasion, without hampering audience involvement, the possibilities are endless. We may even witness a trend of companies producing serials that revolve around their brands, simply because they find that product characterisation gives them greater value for money than conventional advertising. Would Unilever, for example, be tempted to produce a serial that stars Lalitaji, that unforgettable character that helped Surf fight against Nirma, and use it as a medium to reinforce the values that she stands for and the brand she is associated with? Or would Hyundai come up with an Indian version of Knight Rider, starring a talking, thinking Santro?

It may not be long before the Indian market sees such revolutionary marketing tactics. And even today, though the concept of product characterisation is in the initial stage, it should be seen as a potent tool that marketers can use to thwart the remote-empowered viewer. After all, characters in television serials and movies will continue to dominate our lives. And with product characterisation, the same could be true for many brands that are currently struggling to grab the attention of their target audience.

CHAPTER 3

THE CONCEPT OF CATEGORY CATALYSTS (2002)

Price offs, mega discounts, value offers, Buy-2-and-Get-1-Free, buy a packet of tea and get a chocolate free! The current brandscape seems like a plethora of promotions. There are so many of them that the person at the supermarket cash counter forgets what is free with what and how many rupees have to be taken off on that bar of soap. An environment scan leaves one with the feeling that in this era of price-off-driven customer preferences, marketing has been reduced to just finalising the best possible promotional offer.

Establishing brand recall and advertising recall has become extremely difficult due to media fragmentation at one end and information overload for customers at the other. So marketers have resorted to "promotion pep-ups" – the use of promotions to pep up volumes at an unprecedented scale. After all, it helps in swinging the purchase decision right at the point of decision against an array of other brands.

Does it mean that the customer today is defined as one who is merely seeking "more bang for buck," and has reached a stage of brand neutrality against brand preference? Does it mean that realisations from customers will continue to go downhill as marketers are forced to add more and more value-adds to create a semblance of preference for their brands within a defined price range?

Not quite. Let us consider some of the recent phenomena in the world of marketing.

Globally, the men's shaving market was exhibiting a marked shift towards disposable razors. Sleek, convenient and cheap disposable razors epitomised the current 'use-and-throw' attitude. The marketing effort then should be focused on providing the best possible disposables at the lowest possible prize.

And as the market shifted to disposables and then to cheaper disposables, realisations from customers in the men's shaving category would only decline. But besides launching a competitive offering in the disposable segment, Gillette did something totally radical. Armed with relevant customer insights, Gillette created a never-before shaving experience for customers and priced it at an unprecedented level in the market place.

Gillette Sensor, followed in quick succession by Gillette Mach 3, redefined the entire men's shaving category, and through a superior product offering, created a segment for which customers were willing to pay many times over what they paid for ordinary shaving razors. In India, other brands like Super Max rushed in with their own variants. Though priced cheaper than Gillette, even these brands were able to get far better realisations from customers than they had ever got with their ordinary razors. Yes, the right customer insights can result in products, which not only enhance the perceived value of the brand itself but of the entire category in which the brand operates. We can term such brands as 'Category Catalysts.'

Another example: In India, getting a shirt made meant buying a shirt piece or what is popularly referred to as a 'cut piece' at an abysmally low rate. Then the piece is dumped at a neighbourhood tailor who would stitch it cheap. Exactly how cheap was a favourite topic of conversation when a few men got together. There was no sartorial consciousness, and the nuances between a normal versus a button-down collar were hardly understood.

But brands like Louis Philippe, Van Heusen, Allen Solly and Peter England changed all that. They made customers realise that the manner in which they dressed could bring about a change in the way they were perceived by others, and in the way they felt about themselves. Thanks to the category catalysts, not only is the urban market converting rapidly to readymades, but the perceived value of a shirt per se has gone up from Rs. 100 to Rs. 300 even for an unknown brand. Besides enhancing the perceived of the entire category, these brands have also ensured that Indian men look smarter now.

Take a low-involvement category like ball point pens. Reynolds was the standard writing instrument and brands were trying to carve out market share by offering parity products at a cheaper price. Enter Add Gel with the concept of gel pens. Tapping into an undefined customer need, this brand provided a much superior writing experience at a higher price, and quickly built up preference across segments ranging from students to professionals. Consumers are willing to pay for these superior benefits, improving realisations over normal ballpoint pens and once again enhancing the perceived value of the entire category.

Another category is that of toothbrushes. On one end, the marketplace was crowded with a slew of brands with very little to differentiate one from the other. At the other end, customers had little brand awareness about what they were using to brush their teeth with. Most customers purchased toothbrushes like any other commodity with little consideration for the brand name or related benefits.

The only criterion used for brand selection was to purchase the same brand as that of the toothpaste which they used. The priority for most brands in this kind of a marketing scenario was how to offer a product at a lesser price and gain share in the process. Enter, a totally unknown brand called Aquafresh. Establishing the point that toothbrushes also had to be used for brushing gums and then owning the "gentle on gums" platform through the "tomato test" communication, Aquafresh created a market for value-added toothbrushes where none existed. In the process, this category catalyst made customers pay 200 percent more for toothbrushes which were soft and gentle on their gums.

Customers also became aware that they had to check whether their toothbrush was soft or hard. All subsequent activity in the toothbrush market, even from the established brands like Colgate and Close Up, shifted to providing superior and differentiated value to customers at a relevant price.

In a marketing landscape littered with promotional wars, there is potential within each category to provide relevant value to customers and create category catalysts.

CHAPTER 4

AN UNCONVENTIONAL SOURCE OF LEARNINGS ON MAKING A RELAUNCH WORK (2002)

Relaunches are an integral part of marketing strategy and brand presentation. Brands are relaunched on an ongoing basis, claiming more relevant benefits to garner mindshare and create a favourable disposition amongst customers. Another compelling reason for relaunches is to contemporise the brand in terms of its benefits and propositions to the ever-changing needs of customers. And many of these attempts evoke a near-feeble response from the brand's target audience.

At a time like this, when relaunches rarely make a significant impact, there has been one relaunch that has made a gargantuan impression. What's more, the brand, if we may call it one, itself was not something that enjoyed a large recall prior to its relaunch. In fact, it was almost entirely obliterated from public memory; the brand also belonged to a category that was irrelevant in terms of customer desires in today's times.

Clearly, the task at hand was to relaunch a brand that belonged to a defunct category. The brief can be compared to that of trying to revive the general category of, say, long play records and within that category, the almost eponymous His Master's Voice brand in this age of CDs and MP3 players.

What is even more surprising is that those behind this revival are not professional marketers who scan every customer movement with an eagle's eye to spot a segment, a variant or a relaunch opportunity, whether overtly displayed or latent. One of the biggest relaunches in recent times is that of the category of tragic love stories in cinema, and the brand that I refer to is the movie *Devdas*. At a time when cinema tries to be more cool or come across as "happening," either through realistic themes of the underworld or through stories woven around characters who waltz between Shimla and Switzerland at the drop of a hat, *Devdas* is one movie that has been made at least twice over in the past and communicates the theme of unfulfilled, everlasting love, rejuvenating the brand with awesome impact. And those who have pulled this off are director Sanjay Leela Bhansali and his team who are not professional marketers in any sense of the word.

Consider the high impact relaunch of *Devdas* from a marketer's perspective. First, the content of the film in terms of being a tragic tale of unfulfilled love was well known. What's more, the success of its past versions evoked nostalgia from some age groups. However, besides just attracting these audiences, the success of the relaunched version lay in its ability to attract an entirely new audience, thereby broadbasing the target audience. Attracting new segments is one of the reasons for realunching existing brands; *Devdas* has managed to do that successfully.

The other big area where the relaunched *Devdas* scores is in terms of brand experience. The core values of the brand in terms of social era, unfulfilled love and tragedy are well known to audiences. But the lavish and stylised manner adopted for presenting these values adds a new dimension to the brand experience in the relaunched version of *Devdas*. All relaunched brands attempt to provide an enhanced brand experience, but *Devdas* achieves this through the extravagant form that has been used to recount an already well-known story. This experience manages to engage the attention of first-time viewers, besides providing a new perspective as well as a compelling reason for those who have already seen the previous versions to still watch this one.

Another objective of relaunching brands is to contemporise them and remain in sync with ever-changing customer needs. The core values of *Devdas* may not stand the test of relevance today, given the sea change in values. But instead of Devdas ending up being perceived as a no-good loser, the relaunched version manages to highlight a key emotion which is a huge lacuna within the current social structure – that of love being greater than life itself. In an era of divorces at the drop of a hat and ambitions being pursued at the cost of all relationships and ties, *Devdas* manages to evoke the latent need for love amongst today's audiences.

The modification of the female characters is another way of modernising this version. Given the changing status and aspirations of today's woman, women are presented in this version after significantly strengthening their characters. Audiences may ponder over Devdas' motivations, and some may perceive him to be a loser, but the characters played by Madhuri Dixit and Aishwarya Rai will be remembered as strong, assertive women.

Consider another critical area for a successful relaunch: exciting promotions to generate trials. Bhansali and his team have created an unprecedented promotional exercise that ensured enough trials in terms of initial ticket sales for the product. Creating hype by publicising the product as one of the most expensive movies ever made in the history of Indian cinema, *Devdas* ensured enough trials for the product and managed to create an unparalleled wave of curiosity even amongst those who were least interested in themes of this nature.

While there have been remakes by Hollywood of superhits like Star Wars and ET in the past, those have been more in the league of commemorative initiatives riding on nostalgia. Creating an entirely new version and driving it like a brand relaunch is something that this version of *Devdas* has achieved.

There will always be endless debates on whether the hype surrounding the movie was actually worth it and whether it is a classic or just gaudy kitsch unleashed on audiences in the guise of being one of the most expensive movies ever made. But clearly, from a marketer's perspective of creating high impact relaunches that attract new segments, *Devdas* clearly seems to have a lot to offer.

CHAPTER 5

THE SCOURGE OF MARGINAL MARKETING (2004)

Quick, think of any brand of toothpaste, toothbrush or detergent. You may recall the main brand name but what about its variants? If you can't remember those, you're not alone. Try asking the shopboy at your *kirana* store, he's probably not even aware of their existence.

The shop-owner may recollect the names but is likely to politely tell you that they're not in stock at present, or even that the manufacturer has not been able to supply the variations for quite some time now.

It's not just fast-moving consumer goods. Marketers are increasingly facing situations where awareness-building are exercises in futility.

Mass media is no longer "mass," given the level to which it is splintered. Consider the plethora of 24-hour movie, news and music channels with little to differentiate one from the other. Combine that with an ongoing barrage of movies being telecast by local cablewallahs through hundredth-generation, faded VCDs meshed with the most intrusive advertising by local retailers – the result is a mind-numbing experience for customers.

An experience of customers remembering a commercial immediately after viewing is itself an achievement, and day-after recalling of it, unheard of.

In such a situation, how does a product stand out? Most marketers are faced with the constraints of ensuring ongoing growth, that too when some categories are barely growing, and when they have limited/declining budgets.

Then there is the external environment made up of benumbed consumers. While a new template that provides an optimal response in this new, much-transformed environment is required, marketers are coping with the help of **'Brand Incrementalism'** in the meantime.

Brand incrementalism is essentially tweaking and making minor changes in the product or creating new variants with little differentiation. Some of the examples that we encounter on an ongoing basis are:

- **Packaging Modifications**: How often do you see products with minor packaging modifications? The impact in terms of enhanced customer benefit may be minimal or insignificant, but it is one way of staying in the public eye.

- **New and Improved Versions**: Consider the plethora of launches announcing new and improved versions of the product. Again, the enhanced benefits of the new and improved avatar are fuzzy, making it difficult for the customer to comprehend how this version has made a significant difference to his/her life compared to the earlier version. Brands routinely become "new and improved" or "super powered." The race then, is to find the least-overworked adjective; even local colloquialisms are acceptable since they impart a local flavour to the brand. In most cases, this brand incrementalism fails to explain what has imparted it with "great strength" and what was added over and above that "great strength" to make the brand the best ever.

- **Brand Variants**: New variants certainly help in gaining shelf space, but they also confuse the customer. Most consumers cannot recall the prefix or suffix attached to the core brand name for creating this variant. Nor can most of the standard retailers. That is important, since these brands generally get the maximum throughput from these stores, given the current state of retailing. After all, supermarkets and hypermarkets are still an emerging phenomenon. And at the local grocery store, there is generally not enough space available for consumers to see each of the variants, understand their subtle differences and make an informed choice.

- **Changes to the Core Brand**: Generally, these are variations or changes created purely as reaction to competition. Consider the battle in toothpastes. Once it was discovered that the germ-fighting property of toothpastes carried a high consumer impact, the quality became a battleground for all toothpaste manufacturers. In the percentages game that followed, certifications by dental institutes from all over the world attested to even 110 percent germ-fighting ability. And the impact on the consumer? By all accounts, the customer watched from the sidelines as the battle intensified in pitch and tone, and went on to buy his preferred brand anyway.

Such ongoing incrementalism goes largely unnoticed by today's customers. Instead of the routine of brand incrementalism, today brand building and strengthening of brand equity is all about bold, never-before initiatives that make a profound impact on a consumer's lifestyle. And there are proven instances of brands that have taken bold, innovative steps and stayed a step ahead, not of competition, but of their consumer's needs.

A brilliant example of non-incrementalist brand building is Hyundai's approach to the small-car segment. The Korean car company started with the basic premise that even a small car could provide the same or even better level of comfort as a big car. That required a design innovation for the Santro – the unique "tall boy" design. While the design was successful, it was merely the beginning of a slew of never-before innovations from Hyundai, which completely changed consumers' expectations regarding a small car.

The Santro next came up with never-before driving convenience in the form of the first affordable power steering in a small car. And consumers have no trouble recalling that this innovation was called 'the Zip Drive.'

Even as the competition went into overdrive to offer power steering in their vehicles, Hyundai was implementing another radical brand-building strategy – another relaunch. And this was no incrementalist relaunch done after tweaking the shape of the tail-lights or the wipers. The Santro's design was changed in its entirety, in spite of the fact that the earlier version was selling extremely well. Another brand name suffix was created that consumers not only remembered but extremely appreciated – the Santro Xing.

Hyundai is not the only auto manufacturer to behave in such an intrepid manner. Honda took the same audacious route with the Honda City. The earlier design was well established in the premium segment. But instead of tweaking it here and there and falling into the brand incrementalism trap, Honda overhauled the design and created the new Honda City. This was a change driven by the conviction that consumer needs have changed and a contemporary, more economical and more fuel-efficient version is what they now seek. Importantly, this was a change that diverse consumer segments have noticed and understood.

Both the Xing and the new City could have been variants that coexisted with their now "earlier" versions and could have been priced accordingly. Such an incremental strategy would perhaps have been incrementally successful and would have delivered incremental results. But by these brave manoeuvres these brands have enhanced their equity immensely. And that's likely to show up in the brands' impact on customers and stakeholders as well.

Today's rapidly changing consumer and media landscape demands intrepid responses from marketers to make an impact. And the lessons on this are being written by a capital-intensive segment where change is more difficult than in other industries.

CHAPTER 6

THE 360-DEGREE SPIN (2006)

In earlier times, a big-budget Bollywood movie would open on a Friday. You had one of many options. Take a risk, see it over the weekend and find out for yourself how it is; check with a few friends in case they have seen it already; or wait for the first set of reviews to come out in the dailies on Sunday and decide whether the movie merits spending time and money on over the coming weekends.

Now consider the scenario today for some sets of audiences – the movie releases on Friday. By Friday noon, internet portals are brimming with reviews, counter reviews and even audience comments! The reviews scale the whole spectrum from 'Avoid' to 'Must See' and various levels of tolerance in between.

People even have the opportunity to post their own reviews and have online debates.

For audiences that are not net savvy, the instant information sources beyond online have also exploded. No access to the internet? Does not matter. Simply switch on any of the news channels and they will be beaming audience reactions to a movie live after the very first show. Worried about geographical segmentation? You can watch audience reactions from areas as diverse as Madurai and Mahabaleshwar on your television screen. And even if you are not watching television, there is the obsessive-compulsive fingertip disorder – SMS. SMS can reach millions of people divulging the real killers in suspense movies or providing short 'Must See' or 'Must Avoid' reviews in a flash.

Now imagine this same level of information dissemination for all products and services besides cinema and its repercussion on business. It's actually happening.

Take the launch of a new variant from a soft drink company. The trendiest of advertising with some of the hottest and highest ranked celebrities will be developed for a core target of young audiences. The advertising will score very highly on all counts of likeability and relevance. Events will be planned around the launch. And what does the "oogling" generation for whom the drink is intended actually do?

Search on the web and find out that this "hot," "new" variant is nothing but a version that failed miserably in Mexico last year. One blog comment and 25 SMSs are enough to spread the word across many colleges and cities. The advertising works but the variant does not! There have always been discussions about "well informed" customers and now this information wave is cutting across all traditional demographics in terms of age groups, income and socio-economic classifications.

This is a fundamental shift in business and marketing strategy. The first fundamental shift is related to traditional segmentation and customer information processes. Traditional marketing segmentation has relied on demographics, psychographics or a combination of both. For example, demographically, a sewing machine can be marketed to women in the age group of 35–45 with a monthly income of Rs. 8,000. She is likely to be a homemaker, a mother or someone who likes to do things for one's family. While these conventions still hold, there are two distinct sets here – a homemaker who is an enabled "information seeker" and uses diverse information sources, versus one who does not. And the strategy needs to be adapted for both these audiences.

A 30-second-spot during the afternoon soap opera would have worked for housewives relaxing before their afternoon naps. But for housewives who are surfing the net and browsing through all the detailed features of sewing machines available in Japan and Germany, the company's website needs to be updated, not with cursory product details but with product benefits, and give compelling reasons why this product provides the utmost convenience and meets her needs.

And the amount of energy, effort and expertise that the organisation needs to harness in terms of creating and utilising this information source needs to be at the same level as what goes in creating the 30-second commercial, if not more. There needs to be an inbound helpline for answering all queries linked to the sewing machine. And other interaction and engagement options like SMS-based marketing need to be leveraged.

The seemingly endless news channels can also be used to obtain genuine customer and prospect feedback on the product. Like open source software, there is also the possibility of customer engagement in the development stages of the product itself – a whole new form of product development focus groups.

This also means a significant shift in the traditional communication development process. Core propositions have to be communicable effectively across diverse media from a commercial to an internet banner to a search engine text communication. After all, a customer may start by using a search engine to seek a product, then move on to receiving a friend's comments on the product through SMS and then see a hoarding for the product. The whole journey from awareness to interest to desire to action to satisfaction has become non-linear and random.

A clear example of harnessing this randomness to complete advantage has been achieved by BMW. To appeal to the Blackberry-addicted, internet-embedded successful executive, and yet communicate all the core values of BMW, the company created a series of films by noted directors like John Woo and made them available on its website – a trendsetting initiative that created a never-before buzz for the brand amongst its younger demographic target. It also enabled communication of brand values and customer engagement that a standard 30-degree spot could never have achieved.

Businesses need to build customer propositions that can compete globally, and also explain why they are tailored for specific ethnographic audiences. And they need to leverage the umpteen information sources available to today's customers. Think about it. The iPod has reached a level of near "universal awareness" and is "universally desired," and Apple has achieved this by spending hardly any amount on conventional mass media advertising.

The 360-degree brand experience has long been a part of our business lexicon. This may be the best time to invest in getting it right and reaping the benefits.

Part 2

POST SMARTPHONE ERA INSIGHTS

CHAPTER 7

THE EMERGING AND HIGHLY RELEVANT CONCEPT OF 'CUSTOMER INTERACTION MODELS' (2009)

The recession is already upon us. Take a look at all predictions and emerging ways to manage this downturn. The essence of the inputs provided stays the same. Manage costs extremely well and make the marketing budgets work harder by finding relevant media opportunities. Look at innovative ways to drive growth through new segments and new products. Marketing budgets are already being sliced, diced and overanalysed.

The aspect of cost management has manifestations across the entire organisation. The focus on managing costs of raw materials, inventory and process improvement will continue. Additionally, companies are trying to cut manpower across the board besides moving towards more technology-driven and less human-based cost saving approaches.

This rationalisation of manpower and focus on cost management can have severe repercussions on the overall standing of the organisation across all its metrics from top-line growth to profitability and market share. Let us consider some of our own common experiences while dealing with organisations in various sectors.

You walk into an electronics store to evaluate different kinds of refrigerators and buy one that best suits your needs. First, compared to the number of prospective buyers in the store, there are not enough store assistants as the company has streamlined on this cost. When you finally get the attention of the store assistant, the person is a novice who does not have enough knowledge about all the refrigerator brands and their benefits. Armed with that limited knowledge, the person does not even try to find out the size of your home, the size of your family and the price range, besides any other specific needs that you are looking at. You have to make all the choices and decisions practically on your own, without a fair sense of whether your selection actually meets your needs.

Take a sports store as another example. The display is excellent, and the retail environment has a terrific look and feel. You walk in to try and find running shoes that suit your running style. The shop assistant is a part-timer hired at a low salary for the company to save costs. The person does not even know the difference between trail running and normal running, besides having no idea whether your running style demands more cushioning or stability. You end up making your own choice which may be suboptimal, and that results in either foot injuries or back problems later.

Let's also look at large format supermarkets. FMCG companies keep launching variants of their core products to attract different segments. You are perplexed whether the conditioner variant mentioned will help to straighten frizzy hair while retaining hair colour. The information on the packaging is indicative but not elaborate. You try to seek help. Except the crowded cash counters and the attendants who replenish empty store shelves, there is no one around. The cash counter attendants know nothing and are too busy managing the crowds checking out. Having purchased the product anyway, you call their toll-free number. You are guided to an outsourced remote call centre where the only advice provided to your question is an email id where you can send your query and wait for the company to respond.

These common examples, which all of us have experienced in different forms and magnitude during various shopping experiences, form the backbone of what is called the 'Customer Interaction Model.'

The Right Resource at the Right Place

The Customer Interaction Model begins with an end-to-end mapping of how the brand interfaces with the customer at various customer touch points such as different forms of retail outlets, call centres and websites.

Management of the Customer Interaction Model entails deployment of the right level of resources at each of these touch points. These resources should be knowledgeable and available to provide customers all relevant inputs about the solution which a brand provides to address each customer's specific needs. As the examples above illustrate this, the Customer Interaction Model can be used across categories from services to consumer durables to fast-moving consumer goods.

It is critical for organisations to commence understanding this Customer Interaction Model for their products and services and to intensively focus on this aspect. As the recession deepens, customers will become extreme value seekers. They will want to know and consider everything about the product in advance before shelling out their money and making a purchase. And brands or companies which are able to clearly and simply explain to customers how their products meet the specifically stated needs of customers will gain market share, while brands which do not do this explicitly will end up losing share.

Technology Revolution

The technology revolution is another reason for companies to commence intensively mapping and driving their Customer Interaction Models. At one end, technological advances are happening at a rapid pace, and many of these are really stupendous. At the other end, most customers are very basic users when it comes to technology, and need products and services simplified. They also need very clear answers to their basic questions.

A brand may have some fantastic features, but if these are not elaborated upon properly at the retail outlet, those features will not provide any distinct advantage to the brand. Imagine a technology feature that allows for sharper rendering of images in digital cameras automatically with every click. While being customer friendly, if the sales person at the retail outlet cannot explain this feature, then the product development edge and the brand's ability to command a premium for this feature is lost.

The pressure on costs is another compelling reason why companies need to map and manage their Customer Interaction Models. Companies may end up cutting back on sales and service staff or providing insufficient training inputs to their sales and service staff or even hiring suboptimal sales and service staff due to cost pressures, thereby having a huge adverse impact on their Customer Interaction Model. Even prior to the recession, the quality of sales and service staff in different categories has had huge room for improvement. Organisations will need to ensure that these staff can genuinely understand customer needs, provide the right solutions, clearly explain product benefits and guide customers towards prompt redress of any issues and complaints.

Imagine walking into an electronics store to buy a laptop. You are greeted by an assistant immediately. She understands your budget, your computer usage needs, and your maintenance requirements and suggests two models. Then she explains the salient differences between these two models. You make your choice. She even provides a financing plan based on the upfront payment and the instalment that you can afford. She explains the effective interest rate charged. She also provides an extended service and maintenance warranty. Finally, she offers to get the laptop delivered, with the operating system installed, and she offers to provide training on the operating system.

Naturally, your choice is made easily. Such a shop assistant will not be a low-cost resource, and besides qualifications, such a person will also need loads of product training. But the benefit of these costs in terms of sales generated per resource will be huge. Companies need to be careful in not taking cost-cutting approaches for such resources, but actually investing in them during a downturn.

What's Apple Chewing On?

A company which has already been doing this is Apple. Apple has stacked up huge resources at the point where customers interact and engage with Apple's innovative and advanced technology products. At the Apple Stores, rather than salespeople peddling Apple products, there are immensely unique concepts which have been implemented. For example, there is a concierge to meet and greet customers and understand their requirements. There are specialists who conduct free workshops on Apple's hardware and software products. There is a Genius Bar where customers can interact with Apple-certified 'Geniuses' to diagnose issues related to their Apple software or hardware. These Geniuses also suggest repair and replacement alternatives. Apple has put the same level of focus on its Customer Interaction Model as it has on its product, thereby imparting a whole new dimension to how the brand interfaces with its customers.

High-end cosmetics companies have also been stacking up resources using their Customer Interaction Models, as much as they have been investing in product development and above-the-line brand building. They have invested in shop-in-shop formats within multi-brand department stores equipped with trained beauticians who can check skin tones, explain the benefits of the variants and even show how to use certain products.

While innovations and new product development are good measures to counter a recession, they also have a development cycle. Companies need to continue investing in above-the-line brand building and focusing on their core brand values. Additionally, an approach of understanding how the brand and product interact with customers at various other interaction points and then stacking up adequate resources to optimise these opportunities needs to be pursued. This will enable companies to clearly communicate product benefits or convert customers and provide efficiencies while enabling them to gain share from the extreme value seekers that customers are bound to become during these recessionary times.

CHAPTER 8

BEAT THE BLUES! UPBEAT BUSINESS MODELS DURING AN OVERALL DOWNTURN (2009)

As the downturn deepens, marketing budgets that have never kept up with the splintered media environment nor with media cost inflation are now under serious scrutiny, if not halved already. Marketing departments are under severe pressure to cut media costs and reduce overall departmental costs.

Businesses are also reeling and working through ways to manage their top lines and bottom lines in an environment where the news only gets more depressing each day. Existing business models seem increasingly inadequate to tide over this current crisis. Besides stemming any declines in their existing sales, business managers are attempting to figure out ways to sustain momentum and are seeking new avenues for profitable growth.

Consumers have already started tightening their purse strings and are looking at ways of deriving economic benefits across their entire continuum of spend requirements. This is already manifesting itself in various forms of customer behaviour related to deferring of non-essential purchases, travelling less frequently, seeking savings in essential purchases and increasing one's savings rate on an overall basis.

While economies and businesses struggle, and consumer sentiment stays pessimistic, there is significant room for innovation and business building within this downturn environment.

Despite the Recession…

Let's look at businesses which were born and have been immensely successful during a recession in one of the world's most expensive countries and one of its largest markets for luxury goods.

Mention the word Japan, and the primary connotations are 'expensive' and 'quality.' Japanese consumers are often touted as being exceedingly brand-and quality-conscious. These customers are known to pay two or three times the normal price for prestigious brand names and for perceived quality. In a country where a meal can set one back $200 per head, the recession of the last 10 years has created many distinct and hugely successful businesses. These businesses which have flourished during the period that is now universally acknowledged as the "lost decade" of Japan provide valuable insights on how business models can evolve and be strengthened during a recession.

The Japanese currency has always been maintained at a level which works on a multiple of 100 against the US dollar. And the country is notorious for being expensive, consistently making it to the list of one of the most expensive countries in the world. A 100 yen in Japan is enough to buy just one can of Coke from the omnipresent vending machines dotting Japan's urban landscape.

With that perspective, during the recession of the nineties, '100 Yen Stores' started emerging in Japan. Walk into any of these outlets and one can get a whole range of items ranging from houseware to cutlery to stationery to batteries to hanging hooks to buckets to domestic toolkits and even food. There is one guiding principle: each and every item are priced at 100 yen only or the equivalent of one standard coin. So one can get a useful toolkit for home use for the price of a Coke can in Japan. And stretching the affordability boundary, even in Indian terms the cost of each item is a mere Rs. 50, something which Indians on an Indian salary can also easily afford. With Japan's widespread perception of being expensive, this level of affordability is truly astounding.

The 100 Yen Store concept tapped into a changing consumer psyche, which, scarred by the recession, was increasingly seeking value options besides its traditional 'high price, superior brand and high quality' approach. And, customer sentiment was undergoing a significant change because a whole generation of young people had grown up in a recessionary environment and were seeking a value-based shopping approach versus the 'high price and quality' approach of the older generation. The concept risked being perceived as downmarket and "cheap" in this country of common place high-end retail, but instead evolved to become an integral part of the shopping circuit with a huge appeal for the 'raised in recession,' value-seeking, younger segment.

With more than 3,000 items per store, there is a whole range of items which are not found at conventional high-end stores in Japan. The range of items has obviated the 'Footfalls without Fruition' factor with most people walking into these stores finding something useful and walking out with at least one item purchased. And they do this by using just one standard 100-yen coin, earning these stores the nickname of 'Single Coin Stores.'

To scale this concept further, the stores started experimenting with different ranges of merchandise based on the demographic profile of the store location. At present, there are an estimated 1,000-plus such stores in Japan growing at the rate of more than 200 stores a year. This provides customers with a reason to visit different stores in different locations besides their own neighbourhood 100 Yen Store.

The underlying business model driving this phenomenon is simple. Source items on a massive bulk basis from cheap sourcing locations such as China and Brazil. Also look for items which are immensely useful, such as clips to hang washed clothes or household tool kits with hammers and spanners, which are either priced significantly higher at branded retail outlets or do not have any major branded equivalents.

The concept can easily be adapted to the Indian retail environment as an 'All items at one price store.' Stocking a huge and relevant range is achievable because neighbourhood retail formats are already well-versed with stocking a range of items in small spaces. And there are a huge number of local producers with competitively-priced items, but a lack of brand building and distribution capabilities. Add the two, and there could be a breakthrough business model that will benefit Indian consumers as well as local producers during this downturn.

Low Price, High Quality

Another successful business that has successfully tapped into the emerging 'value-seeking' versus 'brand-conscious' psyche of Japanese consumers is the clothing brand Uniqlo. Uniqlo adopted the 'speciality retailer of private label apparel' model, producing their own clothing and retailing it through its exclusively branded retail stores. Its guiding principle is to provide fashionable, high-quality clothes at the lowest possible market prices. Again, instead of being looked down upon, shopping at Uniqlo outlets is considered trendy and happening. The stores provide quality and fashion which is affordable, and the outlets have displays and merchandising which is comparable to any medium range apparel brand globally.

For the 'raised in recession' generation, these outlets have become destinations, while the wide range of clothing appeals to all demographic segments in Japan.

Uniqlo also creates huge 'reason to visit' through unique designs and collections for different seasons and has even launched collections by renowned and upcoming designers. Naturally, the fundamental value is never compromised, and the garments are always at the lowest possible prices. The strategy of affordability and rapid renewal of their product range also results in enhancing the purchasing frequency at their outlets.

The business model again relies on using China as a manufacturing base, with tremendous focus on quality control and designing. The Uniqlo chain has grown to over 750 stores in Japan and has also expanded internationally to locations such as the UK, China, Hong Kong, the US and South Korea.

Retailing of branded apparel that provides huge value and is also trendy, fashionable and hip is another huge opportunity across India.

Tokyo Disneyland is another destination that continues to grow successfully during Japan's recession. Their success is attributed to two factors: it is an accessible family destination which Japanese families love visiting, and it is a place of happiness – a destination which makes people forget their worries and enhances their joys.

Think about the opportunity of developing such destinations in India. Besides the "happiness" factor, the concept can also be augmented to include the "wellness" factor. Yoga and natural healing can have tremendous appeal during these stressful times.

In India, the recessionary environment also provides immense opportunities for developing business models in underpenetrated segments. Insurance is one example. The need for security is significantly enhanced during uncertain times. Insurance companies can tap into this need by creating innovative products like unemployment insurance or healthcare-linked insurance besides providing a multitude of options within conventional life insurance products.

The success of these business models during a recessionary period in a mature market such as Japan proves that there is a huge opportunity to create radical business models in a downturn. The key is to provide customers genuine value, be perceived as hip yet accessible, and also provide customers joy and optimism.

Now let us wait for India's inherent innovative and improvisation prowess to be unleashed during the downturn here.

CHAPTER 9

THE GROWING POWER OF "BRAND BUZZ" AND "BRAND CHATTER" (2009)

The challenges of brand building continue to multiply exponentially. Consumer behaviours are changing drastically, making marketers revisit and reconsider the standard tenets of segmentation. The media environment is one where layers and layers of complexity are getting added each day.

Customers have transformed. From the glory days where consumers were mere recipients of marketing messages, converting these into perceptions, consumers are now active participants in media. The extent of customer "expression," powered by blogging to Facebooking to the recent and rapidly-increasing tweeting phenomenon, are changing the rules of marketing every day.

How do marketers create a buzz in this environment to strengthen their brands? The word 'buzz' encompasses a lot of things from the attention-grabbing properties of the brand, to the impact of the brand, and finally to word of mouth or what we can say "non-paid media" cascading impact that it can generate. Based on my own observations, let us look at some of the brands which have successfully harnessed the "buzz" factor in recent times in a developed and mature market like Hong Kong.

Consider the launch of the global fashion retail brand H&M in Hong Kong. A European fashion retailer popular for its trendy and ever-changing designs marked by affordability. This fashion retailer had an arduous task as Hong Kong is swarming with apparel retailers who provide a range that appeals to every conceivable demographic and psychographic segment. Add to that the fact that Hong Kong's retail environment is extremely crowded with a large number of malls many of which have become a habit for customers in this city starved for space and bursting at its seams.

Well-established apparel brands operate across all points of the pricing and affordability spectrum. Rather than opening their first store in a mall and becoming another retail face in an already crowded environment, H&M opted for a standalone store, and that too in the heart of Central, Hong Kong's business district. This standalone store strategy significantly helped in establishing brand awareness and creating curiosity about H&M even before the store had actually opened. Much more than what conventional mass media print advertising may have achieved.

Another challenge would have been to quickly establish some brand association. The strategy was to focus on the segment that loves shopping, and more importantly, the segment that loves talking about shopping – women. H&M chose to advertise their brand by linking it to pop icon Madonna, someone who appeals to women across all age groups.

But the celebrity association went a lot beyond mere brand endorsement. The fashion retailer actually got Madonna to design a whole collection for them. And the launch campaign commenced by showing Madonna, the clothes designed by Madonna and an even more important variable – the pricing.

Finally, for the launch, H&M announced that there would be a limited number of trench coats and sunglasses signed by Madonna, offered on a first-come-first-served basis. The pre-launch buzz about this availability reached such limits that more than a thousand odd people waited for the store to open its doors to Hong Kong overnight. By continuously refreshing their collection, associating with major designers and never losing their focus on price, H&M is thriving in a developed fashion market like Hong Kong and is adding more stores.

Another example of the buzz factor is the cotton bag that has the statement "I am not a plastic bag" emblazoned on it. It was created by London-based designer Anya Hindmarch. The bag was designed with a noble objective of making consumers use less plastic bags for their grocery shopping and saving the environment – a designer handbag that made a statement about the user and was available at probably one percent of the price of normal designer handbags.

Fashion magazines started covering this bag and giving it huge exposure, significantly enhancing the "must have" quotient. To accentuate this further, it was announced that only a limited number of originals had been produced and only a portion of those produced would be sold in Hong Kong. Again, thousands of customers lined up on the day this bag went on sale. The bag, costing only HK$ 120 or around Rs. 600, became a hugely coveted object selling at a premium many times over its original price.

Before the financial tsunami struck, the Beijing Olympic Games was the biggest event of 2008 in China and in Hong Kong. Bank of China, one of the major banks in Hong Kong and China, harnessed the buzz potential of this event in a unique and unconventional manner which created a huge must-have effect for the product it created. As a currency-issuing bank in Hong Kong, Bank of China issued four-million-odd currency notes commemorating the Olympic Games. These bank notes were lapped up for seven times their face value as customers simply wanted to frame them as a memory of the unique event.

McDonald's is another brand that continues to harness the buzz factor on an ongoing basis to ensure repeated footfalls into their outlets. Their creative use of unique giveaways with Happy Meals helps them to attract their core audience of children who love to get these ever-changing collectibles. Recently, they went one step further in Hong Kong. The standard for retail stores in Hong Kong is the ubiquitous Seven Eleven chain of convenience stores. The brand name actually stands for the time that these stores stay open from seven a.m. in the morning to eleven p.m. at night. Most McDonald's outlets in Hong Kong are now open 24 hours a day, seven days a week.

While all this has happened in Hong Kong, one cannot help noticing that brands are also harnessing buzz power at home in India. Tata Tea created a huge amount of buzz recently with its 'Jaago Re' campaign, encouraging India's youth to participate in the electoral process. By doing this, they have perhaps redefined the awakening attributes of tea and encouraged millions to vote for stability and progress.

CHAPTER 10

MAKING SENSE OF THE FINANCIAL CRISIS AND LINKED FUNDAMENTAL ACTIONS (2009)

The current economic environment is confounding, to say the least. Forecasts about the unemployment rate continue to receive worldwide press coverage. Estimates indicate that the US unemployment rate could touch 9.7 percent, while in Hong Kong this rate could reach a record 8 percent of the working population. Another forecast from the UN mentions that more than 50 million people or more. While all this news is creeping in, the stock markets continued to rise upward in May after posting gains in March and April. The media has been trying to provide insights to help the common man to make sense of all this. But figuring out the real issues, comprehending the fundamental drivers behind these issues, and fixing them seems to be emerging as a real challenge. Besides varied opinions on when the recession will actually end, another critical aspect that needs a lot more discussion than the current levels is what will cause this recession to end. And, what will the new global order look like? Besides all these areas which need a huge amount of deliberation, another way to look at the recession is to simply consider it as a radical opportunity. Think about the current situation as a chance to make some fundamental changes in the economic and financial systems of the world with far-reaching impact on our future. Let's not consider ways and means to simply get out of the current recession.

Rather let's use this period to make revolutionary and progressive changes that could perhaps end up having a huge positive impact in the post recession world order. As a corporate citizen and a media consumer reading about the crisis as it unfolds and the counter measures being considered, I am throwing up some radical alternatives for the emerging world order.

The first radical approach is related to unemployment. Besides the rate of unemployment, an aspect about the current levels of unemployment that needs a deeper understanding is the structure underlying the current unemployment rate. Simply put, we need to understand more about how much of this unemployment rate comes from college educated or post graduate, high earning individuals who, during good times, may have been earning incomes in the high median ranges. Unemployment within this group will have a huge impact on consumption patterns, employment opportunities and the whole path to recovery. It is obvious that the crisis is having a serious impact amongst many qualified and experienced professionals as well as managers. A lot of bright minds involuntarily idled.

A related issue as this crisis unfolds is how these minds can be deployed productively for the good of the global economy. The worsening crisis in developed nations has serious ramifications in the developing and underdeveloped economies. Poverty reduction programmes in developing countries will not meet any of their planned objectives in 2009. This is where the opportunity could lie in terms of making rapid developmental strides for the whole global economy. Besides finding ways of funding, the bright idle minds can be put to use for resolving some of the problems of the developing world.

The first area where a lot of bright minds can be productively occupied related to funding programmes for malnutrition and poverty. Financial engineering and creative financial methods used simply as greed satiating vehicles have played a significant role in creating the current crisis. But purpose-driven financial engineering may just help to win many battles and perhaps the war against poverty and malnutrition. Whole new approaches and economic models can be developed to conquer these issues which continue to plague the developing world and have a huge impact on global economic growth as well as global human capital. Additionally, issues like global warming and the global water crisis are threatening the entire world. Financial engineering can be applied for a purpose to create unique funding solutions to drive alleviation programmes and build unprecedented scale for these initiatives. After all, the world is waiting for the next big thing in cause-related finance after microfinance.

Another globally under-resourced area is education. Teaching standards, education linked infrastructure, and entire education models can also do with a lot of upgrading across the world. Bright minds can again evolve cheaper and more efficient means of access to education across the world. And many can become teachers themselves, imparting education across their chosen part of the developing world. Let them choose their preferred part of the globe and grade from elementary school to post graduate institutions.

Billions of dollars are also being poured to bail out America's beleaguered auto industry. Instead of pouring in this money to simply save companies from financial collapse, these funds could actually be utilised towards reconfiguring the auto industry towards making environmentally-friendly cars only. A step that, in the future, can be as good for the environment as much as it is a lifeline for the auto industry. Taking that a step forward, a large proportion of these funds could be used to create public transport networks which the United States sorely lacks. Asia has many positive lessons on the benefits of creating massive public transport networks. Places like Japan are pollution free, are not massive consumers of energy, and their public transport networks are hugely profitable.

As banks and financial institutions attempt to survive the current credit environment and shed a huge number of jobs, the opportunity to create significant employment opportunities within this sector is another area that needs to be explored. Starting from collecting resources for accumulated debt, the financial sector can also take this opportunity to refocus from complex financial instruments.

Customers will increasingly need debt management and cash flow planning advice. These are the same customers who in good times were users of wealth management and investment advisory. From basic lending products to even debt restructuring and post bankruptcy management, a huge range of innovative products and services are required from the financial services industry to help consumers tide over the current crisis. All of these can generate a fair amount of employment opportunities.

The end state that some of this radical approach to the crisis can help create is one which fundamentally helps us in creating a better future. Every crisis, as they say, is a hidden opportunity. And there are many million opportunities waiting to be articulated and executed, besides some of the approaches mentioned above…

CHAPTER 11

THE GREATEST GENERATION? (2009)

What is the best economic model in the new post-financial-crisis world? Economists might find their answer in an unlikely place: the experience of the Indian diaspora. The generation of middle-class Indians who left home in the 1960s and 1970s has achieved success across various industries around the world. Thus, the economic environment and upbringing that shaped them warrant a close look.

Save, Then Spend

The concept of consumer banking did not exist in 1970s India. The role of banks was to channel funds received from customers to finance industrial growth. Even mortgages were available only through one national institution with extremely stringent lending criteria.

While this created many economic challenges, it encouraged a unique form of customer behaviour. Households were focused on savings, both in general and for special items. For example, the way to buy a radio or a black-and-white television set was to create an in-house "television family fund," save a certain proportion of the family income over a period of 10 to 12 months, and then buy the appliance. Besides the ability to make debt-free purchases, this created a huge wave of anticipation for the time spent saving. That, in effect, created pride in ownership.

Back then, books were so expensive that there was a hugely profitable business of so-called book-circulating libraries where one could pay a small change and borrow books for a week. And the rare purchased and non-borrowed books were covered with brown paper, neatly catalogued and cherished for years.

Items such as watches and pens were once-in-a-lifetime purchases or stretched further to be heirlooms bequeathed across generations. Watches were the most expensive wedding gifts, and it was not surprising to see two generations winding the same hands of time. Pens also brought pride; entrepreneurs liked to expand businesses by signing agreements with pens used by the founder of the business.

Agricultural growth compensated for this lack of consumption of goods and services, resulting in the Indian economy growing across cycles at 3 percent – steady but measly.

Education Matters

Middle-class families in urban and semi-urban India focused immensely on education. The education system largely comprised of public schools, and had inherent weaknesses, from the quality of teachers to the availability of textbooks. Chemistry labs might have lacked any apparatus, and soccer balls might have deflated. But even within this environment, families placed a huge emphasis on education. Leisure activities and sporting activities were secondary, ignored to focus on excelling first at high school, then college and finally at postgraduate programmes.

Given the state of the country, everybody wanted to become an engineer to help develop the country's infrastructure. Others wanted to become key players in the country's starved healthcare system as doctors. It helped that these were the best-paying professions at that time (and it would help later that they were in demand, globally). With limited seats in good colleges, the competitive prowess of a whole generation was also strengthened. With its focus on education, the generation helped create India's technology prowess. The army of successful non-resident Indians that went abroad sought to further their education, often duly armed with scholarships.

Corporations Prided Themselves on Being "Good Corporate Citizens"

The prime purpose of companies was to provide goods and services to a scarcity-prone economy and to create employment opportunities; profit was a by-product. Naturally, salaries were low, but the real compensation was priceless – a huge sense of job security. Employees were also intensely loyal, and it was not uncommon to find individuals who spent their whole working life in just one organisation. Companies formed "colonies," so there was no separation of work and family life. Most of these organisations were owned by entrepreneurs, given the incipient state of capital markets.

Survive with a Smile

The first television set acquired in one household quickly became the whole building's. Car pools were auto-created. Sharing was second nature in an economy marked by scarcity. There were no instant personal loans or card limits available. Family and friends filled this void. Someone in urgent need of a scooter to manage a sales job would borrow money from their near or distant family members, and would be obligated to repay this interest-free loan as soon as possible, given their strong family ties.

The lack of medical insurance meant that the fees and charges for emergency medical services had to be coughed up in advance, and the burden largely fell on family, friends or even neighbours if there was not enough cash in the household. With no structured employee loan programmes, employers routinely doled out cash to needy employees with barely any interest. The lack of access to any form of consumer finance was fundamentally unhealthy, but a necessary offshoot was the strong sense of helping and sharing that it created.

CHAPTER 12

MALLIFYING THEM WITH CHOICE (2009)

The "mallification" (a coined term) of India's urban and semi-urban areas has begun in earnest. Shopping malls are sprouting up across the board, and the unrealised potential of malls is being discussed in a variety of forums. Every suburb in the major towns boasts of one or two major malls if not more, and for those suburbs that that do not have one as yet, there are malls under development.

Malls have become the new landmarks. People offer directions with reference to the location of a certain mall. Real estate agents and companies charge a premium for buildings located near malls. Malls are also the new hangout for the "hip set." They are on the way to becoming an accepted element of today's urban lifestyle.

Many factors have lead to the boom in mall development. The fundamental driver is, of course, India's economic growth, which has resulted in increased incomes and higher standards of living, particularly in the urban areas. The huge untapped opportunity in organised retail is another factor.

The easy availability of credit, driven by the huge number of credit cards in circulation, combined with on-the-spot instalment programmes, is another factor. Factors like the lack of destinations for families to shop, have a meal and amuse themselves are also driving the development of malls, where families can spend an entire day out shopping, watching a movie and grabbing a bite. There has also been a change in the consumer mindset, particularly amongst the younger generation, that is keen to experience what life has to offer and is willing to spend.

Mall development is at a nascent stage in India, where the key priority is simply to achieve penetration. Footfalls are easy to get because of the novelty of the concept.

But challenges have started emerging. The completion of some malls is getting delayed as developers are unable to attract the planned investments due to the recession. Brands facing cost pressures are either withdrawing altogether from malls or renegotiating rentals, affecting mall profitability. As customers cut back, malls are attracting "free footfalls" that do not translate into sales.

An Evolving Concept

Given the current scenario, the challenges for malls will only increase once the category evolves to a stage of early maturity. How will malls sustain themselves once the novelty wears out and competition becomes more intense? How do malls ensure loyalty during a recession?

I detail below some of the concepts that I have observed and experienced in a mature market like Hong Kong that have led to the ongoing growth of these malls even during the current recession.

The first concept is to match the range of outlets, brands, food choices, parlours, health clubs and other facilities available in the mall with the micro-market within which the mall operates. A micro-market is the surrounding area within which the mall attracts a large section of its clientele.

Malls that operate in low-income areas have a larger range of "value" brands and a small set of "premium" brands. Malls located in higher income areas have a wider range of luxury brands and designer outlets and very few "value" brands.

Malls that are located in office-dominated areas with a few residences ensure that they provide sufficient variety for after-work and lunch-hour shoppers/eaters, in addition to creating events and promotions to draw in the residential crowds during the weekends.

Malls that are located next to five-star hotels exude similar levels of luxury as that enjoyed by the tourists and business travellers staying in the five-star hotels. This ensures that the mall becomes the primary shopping destination for guests staying at the hotels. For example, the IFC Mall and the Pacific Place Malls located adjacent to properties such as the Four Seasons, the Conrad and the JW Marriott.

The approach of focusing on certain market segments has also resulted in malls carving out an identity of their own over the years and standing for some unique attributes. There are malls that stand for a range of beauty products and salon services. Malls such as the IFC Mall provide exclusive beauty products combined with well-trained beauty advisers. They also have top-line salons and innovative spa options in the malls.

There are malls that have developed "kid friendly" attributes. These malls are stroller friendly and have a number of play areas for kids. They also have a range of toy and apparel stores for babies and kids. Even the restaurants in these malls have special "kids meals," besides baby seats and other such accessories. Malls such as Megabox, Times Square and Westwood Plaza are known for being kid-friendly, with play areas, skating rinks and baby-changing facilities everywhere.

Some upscale malls have built on the "uniqueness" attribute. While brands may be available across different malls, these malls have a reputation for selling distinctive collections from a particular a brand. As an example, Puma may have brand stores across many malls, but only some selected malls feature its exclusive Black Collection.

The Landmark Mall in Central has designer collections from Dries Van Noten to Furla to Ermenegildo Zegna that are the latest and exclusive. The Elements Mall has brands such as Bals Tokyo and Mulberry, which are available only at this mall.

A supermarket chain such as Citysuper stocks "organic" and "international" merchandise such as Japanese products, and fruits and groceries imported from all over the world and a range of organic products.

"Home-focused" is another attribute that malls have built as a standout feature. Such malls feature a range of home furnishing brands from different parts of the world, some of which have a single store only in that mall. These malls are able to attract home owners, home-makers and the entire set of "home proud" families.

"Electronic malls" feature the latest gizmos and gadgets from computers to games to peripherals. The Golden Computer Arcade is an example of an electronics-focused mall.

Malls have also built on the "discount brands" attribute. Located on the outskirts, these malls provide high-end or premium brands at discounts. Naturally, these are from an older collection and with limited choice, but the discount factor makes people travel long distances. The Citygate outlet mall in Tung Chung is famous for its discounted brands. Building a core attribute that becomes an "owned" property of the mall over a period of time, helps in significantly strengthening the "mall brand," in ensuring ongoing patronage from its core target audiences and in drawing audiences from different parts of the city.

Layouts That Make Sense

Mall layouts that help to maximise both footfalls and conversions are another key factor in ensuring the ongoing sustainability, profitability and success of malls. As an example, cinemas, which attract the highest footfalls in malls, are typically located on the ground floor for ease of access.

Mass market brand stores are also located next to the cinema halls to grab the attention of the cinema-going crowds and to drive conversions. The upscale brands and eateries are located at higher levels to draw select crowds seeking exclusivity and with greater spending power. Based on their unique attributes, different malls adopt different layout formats to provide the right experience and to achieve a higher percentage of conversions.

Loyalty programmes are another driver of mall sustainability in the mature markets. The Elements Mall loyalty programme offers points, parking benefits, and a concierge service. Birthday benefits and pre-sale invitations are also available to the loyalty programme members.

Like everything else in India, it will be interesting to see how the mall category evolves. Also, it will be exciting to watch how these international concepts used by malls to create a competitive edge and drive profitable growth, are adapted in the Indian context to ride through economic cycles.

CHAPTER 13

THE AFTERLIFE OF CATEGORIES AND BRANDS (2009)

The Brand Planet, if we can use that phrase, is littered with cadavers of brands and even entire categories that are deemed to be extinct like the dinosaurs of the past. Ever evolving and radically transforming consumer preferences have contributed to the demise of many brands and categories. Changing social norms have been another factor driving many categories and the brands operating in these categories to their eventual departure from the planet of brands. Technology has been another meteor responsible for driving many brands and categories to extinction. From gramophone records to tape recorders, from radios to pocket transistors, from video cassette recorders to typewriters, there are many categories that have completely lost their relevance in our lives. The brands that made these categories memorable have disappeared. To older generations, brands such as EC TV, Dyanora TV, Murphy Radios, Bush Radios or Panasonic audio cassette recorders made a massive difference to their lives. Now, these brands and categories find their place in nostalgic ruminations and in glorious memories of the past.

But is a technological or a consumer preference shift really the end of a category or of a brand within that category? Is it really the end of the road for brands that have fallen off the radar and have no place in a consumer's current lifestyle? Conversely, is it possible to resurrect some categories that are 'presumed dead' or 'long extinct?'

Is it feasible to provide these categories a new phase of life by changing their appeal or their core attributes? Is it possible for some of the departed brands to come back with renewed vigour and in a different form while retaining their core attributes? Let's look at some of the examples that lend credence to the possibility of category resurrection and brand revival.

Think about wristwatches in the '60s and '70s. These were timepieces of the hand-wound variety that needed frequent and regular winding. And even the automatic watches needed frequent time adjustments. Swiss watches dominated this space, and there were some American brands besides our very own HMT. Also, most of the Swiss brands were not mass-produced on machines, but needed sophisticated assembling with some level of human intervention. Then came the quartz revolution, bringing with it watches that ran on batteries and needed no winding. They even looked slimmer and better with many more design options than the rather plain-looking mechanical ones – watches that were a lot more affordable besides being easy on servicing and care required. The inherent benefits of the quartz movement combined with the advantages of mass production resulted in the market rapidly adapting to quartz watches. Soon quartz watches became the norm in the watches category and operated across all price points and across all consumer segments. Japanese brands such as Citizen and Seiko led this revolution, and many of the Swiss manufacturers had to follow suit. Digital watches extended the affordability of watches even further, and brands such as Casio dominated this space. Given the huge decline in mechanical watches during the eighties, it was easy to conclude that mechanical watches had lost their lustre and consumers certainly did not need a timepiece that required regular winding and servicing when quartz technology needed neither. The category of mechanical watches was rapidly becoming moribund and was likely to be soon forgotten.

Circle to 2009. The quartz watch movement still operates as the standard of the watch industry. But having gone through all price spectrums and a range of design choices, a new set of consumer preferences has emerged. The watch brands that consumers aspire to own or already possess as once-in-a-lifetime acquisitions are brands such as Breitling, Tag Heuer, Rolex, Omega, Panerai, Patek Philippe and Blancpain.

All of these are mechanical watches or automated mechanical watches that have achieved newfound preference as premium and expensive timepieces, items that people desire as a cherished possession. Consumers, after running through the gamut of quartz watches, are rediscovering joy and appeal in these old-fashioned mechanical watches which come with enhanced chronograph functions embedded in them.

These watches required a level of craftsmanship and focus akin to the delicate art of crafting jewellery, and consumers are according the same premium status to these watches as they once did to jewellery. As treasured possessions much like an item of jewellery, consumers not only don't mind regularly getting their exquisite timepieces serviced but look forward to it in the same manner that many car-lovers love washing and polishing their cars on weekends. In Hong Kong, brands such as Rolex actually retail through jewellery stores. And just as how gold can be traded in to get cash, each Rolex model can be traded in after some years of use to get a pre-set amount of cash back.

Yes, mechanical watches have come back at the top end of the watch category and are coveted, looked after and aspired for like items of jewellery. And with rising incomes, all-round economic growth and increasingly globalised lifestyles, mechanical watches have become the new "flash points" of success. James Bond or George Clooney wear an Omega, Leonardo DiCaprio proudly sports Tag Heuer, and John Travolta likes to fly wearing his Breitling. And even in India, mechanical watches are the new aspiration with Abhishek Bachchan sporting an Omega and Shah Rukh Khan strutting around with a Tag Heuer.

An entire category has resurrected itself by moving away from the mass market functionality platform and adding a new layer of premiumness and aspiration by converting its manual construction into an art that is perceived akin to being as precious as fine jewellery.

A remarkable resurrection and transformation. A similar category resurrection is that of fountain pens in recent times. From being mass-use items before being swamped by ballpoint pens, the fountain pen category has been resurrected as a premium category – a pocket ornament that is critical for all personal signatures.

Moving from a category to a specific brand resurrection, consider an icon of the '60s that was born in the UK due to the fuel shortage of the Suez Crisis of 1956. With petrol being rationed, there was little hope for large cars, and so, a product was created that was small in terms of overall size, and yet, optimised passenger and luggage space – the ultimate small car.

The Rover Mini in the UK. By the late '70s, the model had run through its life cycle and was marginalised by the more advanced versions of small cars that were being perfected by other manufacturers. And then BMW brought the Rover brand and relaunched it as the BMW Mini Cooper in 2001. While retaining the same values of the original Mini in terms of its looks, BMW also went in for some fundamental shifts that helped in increasing the value of the brand. Although retaining the concept of optimising space, BMW opted for a small sporting car version. The other major advantage was the BMW brand name prefix which stood for world-beating auto engineering and had a huge premium appeal. Essentially, BMW created a small car that built on the cult following which the original had created, but infused it with the engineering prowess and the premium appeal that only BMW as a brand could provide. And the original Mini was resurrected, but as a premium car that commands a price range comparable to top-end sedans from other manufacturers, with the same zany look and feel of the original. BMW has not just resurrected the Mini, but made it thrive, making it one of the largest selling cars in recent times. Volkswagen also achieved the same success with the relaunched cult car the Volkswagen Beetle.

As these examples prove, brands do have an afterlife. The same applies to entire categories. And in many cases, the afterlife makes the brand or the category even stronger, enabling it to command a premium and significantly increasing the aspirational value of the brand.

Let's take the case of another premium brand: Brooks Brothers, the icon of American ready-to-wear clothing that has been dressing generations of prominent personalities. Its most premium offering is not a silk suit or patent leather shoes. It is a personal tailoring service that commands a premium over all its off-the-rack offerings. And in addition to human made-to-order services, it has infused the concept of tailoring with a technological edge by creating a digital tailor that maps many parts of the human body with precision.

All the corner-shop tailors in India have a huge ray of hope while they are ruing the ever-growing influence of premium readymade garment brands that consumers are increasingly adopting. They may soon discover a glorious future at the end of the readymade product lifecycle with enhanced services such as digital body measurement and instant made-to-order services.

Afterlife can actually be rewarding!

CHAPTER 14

METROPOLIS METRICS LIKE MARKETING METRICS

Let's measure Mumbai (or any other city) to make it more magnificent. (2010)

I recently tested the waters about the brand attributes of Mumbai with some friends in Hong Kong. The two standout positive attributes that emerged were the Sealink and the Sensex. But the downside attributes made a long list – infrastructure, security, ever-increasing traffic, etc. They can be summarised as Slackness, Slowness and Security – the 3 S's of Mumbai.

Hearing this list of rants and raves, I decided to make my own list of metrics by which we Mumbaikars should measure Mumbai on an ongoing basis. While making this list, two questions sprang to mind: Is this how those who govern Mumbai measure where the city is going? And if not, then surely it couldn't be that difficult to organise.

1) Increase in motorable road capacity: To what extent have motorable roads increased in the city? Right now, we only know that the number of cars is increasing across Mumbai as well as across India. The 'motorable roads ratio' has to increase at a faster proportion than the number of cars registered or the number of autos and buses unleashed on those roads.

2) Increase in alternate road connections between focal points of the city: How many flyovers or additional roads/alternate routes connect, say, Lokhandwala Complex to Andheri Station? Multiple routes are crucial for managing traffic congestion.

3) Average peak-hour driving time from Andheri to Churchgate, Borivli to Churchgate, and various other key points in the city; if infrastructure is developing at the same pace as the vehicular population, this time should stay constant. Ideally, this metric should continue to come down as the city's infrastructure improves, but even constancy will make Mumbaikars happy.

4) Percentage of pothole-free roads. Actually, this is a metric that should be dispensed within good time. Most developed cities in the world do not have potholes. Period.

5) Average time since the last repair of roads: Assuming that roads can last for three years, they need to be repaired every three years to ensure that they are fairly maintained.

6) Percentage of the city covered by regularly-routed public transport with regular frequency.

7) Percentage of population covered by regular bus routes. More frequent buses to more locations will make people use public transport more extensively.

8) Amount of bus seats per capita. Do we have ample bus capacity to cater to Mumbai's ever-evolving demographic?

9) Average age of the bus fleet. This is a metric regularly used by airlines. There is no point in running inefficient, polluting monsters that have depreciated three times over or more in a city trying to rapidly modernise.

10) Number of auto rickshaws per capita and number of taxis per capita – a simple one.

11) Auto and taxi upgrade law. Any auto or taxi that is more than 10 years old should perhaps be given permanent residence in a scrapyard.

12) Are there signals within all junction roads, where two or more roads come together? A routine cause of traffic jams is places

where a few roads come together, but there are no signals to manage the traffic flow.

13) Number of tracks and number of trains that have been upgraded, recast or replaced in the last five years. After all, we cannot keep running rusted trains on tracks that were laid out by the British.

14) Number of new tracks and platforms added to make the city rail network more widespread. The local rail system is the city's lifeline but it is operating like an anachronism with old trains running on even older tracks.

15) Local train capacity per capita.

16) Sky trains and underground train projects complementing the rail network with completion timelines of six months. Any international construction company can put up sky trains or metro networks in six months if not less. In my own experience, a private sector metro project that blocks most of an arterial road in the Four Bungalows area has been going on for more than a year, creating massive traffic jams.

17) Increase in power generation capacity annually. This should be tracking to a rate faster than the rate of growth of power consumption, and include variables like the growth rate of new housing activity that requires new connections. It should also be compared with increases in per capita consumption as computers and air conditioners become common place.

18) A reduction in the cost of power-generation-harnessing economies of scale and using more efficient energy sources. The current buzz in Mumbai is that after being taken over by one of India's top private sector companies, the cost of power has skyrocketed to the point of almost doubling rather than getting rationalised.

19) Minutes of power failure in a month per suburb. This should be tracking to zero, which is what it used to be for Mumbai some years ago, when the likes of Kolkata, Chennai, Delhi and Bangalore were reeling under daily two-or-four-hour power cuts.

20) Sewage capacity: Are our sewage systems equipped to handle the normal load of the rapidly-increasing populace besides the vagaries of weather like unnatural rainfall? All questions but no answers backed by facts and figures today.

20) Upgrading sewage systems. A modern city cannot function with a century-old sewage system.

21) Sewage clog alerts: The reason Mumbai is frequently flooded is due to undetected blockages in its archaic sewage systems. Triggers around this event can help in correcting these situations and prevent calamities.

22) Accurate weather forecasts: if meteorologists in other cities can forecast the daily weather with 90 percent probability of occurrence, what algorithms and statistics do we use, where the general level of confidence in the forecast is near zero? If the weather prediction is rain, then people can be assured of a sunny day.

23) Rate of increase in water reservoir capacity: it's still about four lakes. Only prayers to the rain gods can ensure they are filled. If they aren't listening, it's water cuts. Do we need additional reservoirs and storage capacity correlated to population increases? Yes.

24) Percentage of buildings with rainwater harvesting. Rainwater harvesting has proven to be a cost effective and simple way to store water and insure against any failure of monsoons. New construction should mandatorily have this facility, and its penetration should be tracked for older buildings. Perhaps we should even reduce the tax rate for buildings that do this.

25) Number of hospital beds per capita. If computed, this metric will probably make a lot of people sick.

26) Number of policemen per capita and the percentage of the police force equipped and trained for using sophisticated weapons, at least AK47s. Old double-barreled rifles and good ole lathis cannot do the trick anymore.

Currently, one of the few metrics we have is that the average Mumbaikar has a life expectancy of only 57 years. It's time for Mumbaikars to seek metrics around the issues that are causing life expectancy to drastically reduce and to start sharing these to help drive change. After all, Mumbai is still personified by its people: taxi drivers who know the roads in this city inside out, commuters who vacate their seats for women and the elderly, and people who hold ropes for other people trying to walk through the floods and even provide refreshments.

Across the board, the humanitarian spirit of the people and their boundless energy continues to provide spurts of progress. I have listed twenty-six areas where we need to track progress, as the number '26' is embedded in Mumbai's destiny after the July 2005 floods and the November 2008 terror attacks, both on the 26th of the months. I am sure most people probably have 260 or 2600 more issues. Let's develop a scorecard, track it and communicate it to assess progress. Let's measure Mumbai to make it magnificent.

CHAPTER 15

FOUR MCIDLIES AND
A KENTUCKY BAKED VADA, PLEASE (2010)

One emerging perception about India is that it is a 'quantum leap' economy or country – the opposite of a nation where step changes in trends, or product categories happen in line with a country's economic growth. Instead, things that work take off exponentially.

There are many trends and changes driving this perception. The explosion of the cell phone industry because of prepaid cards, affordable handsets, affordable plans, and innovative distribution for instance. Cell phones have become the "main" phone, penetrating across socio-economic groups and surpassing landline penetration. Another quantum leap is the growth of India's auto industry fuelled by small, fuel-efficient cars along with affordable auto loans and topped by the launch of the world's most affordable car, the Nano.

But is it always a good thing? Perhaps not. I can think of one area where a quantum leap could be seriously bad for our health.

During my last visit to India, we all went to eat at a cheap and cheerful South Indian restaurant in Mumbai that we used to frequent many years ago. Simple vegetarian food, extremely reasonable prices and served without any fuss.

On getting there, we should have realised that something had changed when we tried to park. The parking area was full of premium cars and "trendy looking" people of all age groups. After finally finding a space, we walked to the restaurant and realised what was trendy. The old sign board was gone and replaced by some glitzy arches. Globalisation had taken over our friendly neighbourhood all-vegetarian food spot. And naturally, the snazzy fast food place was crowded to the gills. Even getting fries would have meant a 10-minute wait.

I am sure that India is top of the list for expansion and investment by the fast food majors. While growth is tepid in the developed world, India holds massive potential for these companies, given the increase in spending power and emerging globalised lifestyles.

Also, while fast food has a mere functional appeal or is a "craving-fulfilment" mechanism in the developed world, fast food brands have huge desirability and appeal in India, pegging them as near-premium brands. They are destinations, places to hang out, to be seen in, and of course, to eat in for today's global lifestyle aspirants. And the fast food companies are rapidly adapting their menus to suit Indian tastes and adapting to cultural sensitivities.

Now imagine if fast food chains penetrate every geographical corner and all socio-economic groups as fast as cell phones have. While good in terms of job creation and in terms of solid foreign investments, the downside risk of standard imported fast food offers foods that are high in calories, full of processed sugars and low in nutrients, becoming an integral part of the Indian palate.

By now it is clear that Indians have an amazing level of susceptibility to diabetes and to heart disease. Urbanisation, competition and related stress levels are already increasing at a rapid pace. We already have high growth categories in terms of colas, tobacco and alcohol. Taxation and policy measures have not achieved much in terms of containing their growth. Add to this a potent combination of a dietary change in terms of regular fast food consumption, and we have a lifestyle combination that is a time bomb for Indian health. What we want to avoid, of course, is India taking a quantum leap in terms of the prevalence of diabetes and heart disease.

The whole concept of fast food can take a different turn altogether if the fast food majors expand by bringing in products that are driving their growth in global areas. In mature markets, fast food companies are finding growth by introducing low calorie and healthier choices to their menus.

If that becomes the starting point for their growth in India, then we can have a balanced equation in terms of fast food majors tapping into India's vast potential and Indians digging into healthier food choices provided to them, backed by standardised quality and superb hygiene.

Indeed, fast food majors can develop even healthier versions of India's standard offerings that can have appeal not just within India but can also be exported. McIdly or Kentucky Baked-Not-Fried Vadas, the world is waiting for you!

CHAPTER 16

PACKAGING – THE FIFTH P OF MARKETING (2010)

As the world of marketing gets increasingly complex, the four P's of marketing continue to evolve and be redefined. People, Promotions and many other P's have reached a point where they are considered to be part of the core P's that define marketing. While this evolutionary process continues, there is one aspect of marketing that is acquiring a dimension of huge importance. Defined in various ways one could perceive that this one is already a sub-segment of the current P's, and of course there can now be an argument for making this into a standalone P that defines marketing.

Whichever way one looks at it, there is no question that the 'packaging' element of marketing is assuming unprecedented importance in terms of the way that brand values are established in the modern world of marketing and in the way in which brands institute a connection with customers.

Let us first explore some of the reasons why packaging is becoming increasingly relevant within the marketing spectrum. The old model was used to create brand awareness, and then into actual customer action in terms of a purchase. The traditional way was to call this 'Awareness, Interest, Desire and Action' or the AIDA model. Brands built would first be creating awareness about the product through mass media advertising that would reach the defined target audience. Interest and desire would be created through the content of these campaigns that define the desired brand values and also create a need for them in the consumer's lifestyle. Action of course would be spurred at retail outlets through displays, attractive packaging, and of course, promotions.

Now let's consider the current environment where media vehicles that can have all-encompassing status in terms of reach across a defined target audience simply do not exist. And as more and more consumers spend a massive amount of time in the online space, not just as recipients of media but as participants and content creators, building base level awareness is a difficult task. So unlike in the past, where consumers walking into a retail outlet knew all about the brand and came in to make a purchase, now the retail outlet is the point in most cases, where the brand has its first interaction with its defined target audience. Without going into actual percentages, it has been proven across various types of research that a huge proportion of purchase decisions are now made by the consumers at the retail outlet. And this is why packaging assumes a massive strategic importance in terms of being the brand's first and perhaps only interface that can either lead to a purchase decision or not.

The first real requirement from packaging now is to be able to communicate the core values of the brand to the prospect. Think about some simple segments. For instance, a cosmetic product aimed at middle level executives who want to look good. Does the packaging appeal to the target audience at first glance or is it likely to be perceived as a women's product or perhaps a younger men's product? Shape, colour, the brand logo and the messages mentioned in the logo, besides the explanations provided – all become important elements of this mix.

Listing some of the critical factors in terms of what packaging as a critical P in the marketing mix needs to achieve:

- Does the whole package communicate the brand values adequately? A children's soap trying to communicate cleanliness, protection and skin friendliness needs all these values to be reflected in the packaging.

- Is the packaging relatable to the brand's defined target audience? Again, a brand appealing to the elderly needs to have a mature look to its packaging and not end up looking trendy and young.

- Are the benefits of the product adequately brought to life visually in the way the packaging looks and in terms of the explanations provided? Think about a hair gel. The packaging needs to make the brand look slick to draw a young man wanting to buy it. The benefits of using gel need to be brought out on the packaging to generate trials. A crucial point because the whole task of attracting category entrants for a host of new and never-before-used products has now fallen on the packaging itself.

- Benchmark the packaging against competing brands in the same category that are likely to be present in shop shelves. Does the packaging standout and is it significantly different in terms of its attention-grabbing properties against other players?

- A bigger level of benchmarking is not just against other players but against brands in different categories having same or similar-sized packaging.

- Finally, just as core products continue to be improved with better and never-before benefits, for e.g., new and improved versions of washing powders, the packaging also needs to be reinvented to be perceived as innovative and relevant.

Once the packaging has led to a purchase, there is another imperative that packaging needs to achieve, and that is in the area of usability. How friendly is the packaging in terms of opening and accessing the product? Across categories we struggle while trying to open multiple layers or simply struggle to get to a slice of packed bread. Making this access configuration exceedingly customer friendly is vital. Post purchase, this is the first level where the customer is trying to access the core product, and if the packaging makes it onerous or complicated, then the customer's decision to reuse the brand in a parity-offering scenario will be impacted.

Having provided product access in a neat manner, the ongoing usage should also be facilitated through packaging. While travelling,

I have frequently experienced situations where my shaving foam has run out while I am attempting to shave quickly before a meeting. Naturally, one thinks why can shaving foam cans not be transparent for customers to check how much is remaining or even have indicators so one does not have to experience an early morning crisis while trying to catch a timeline in a strange place. All of us have many and more such instances on how packaging can be improved.

Even for an iconic product like the iPod, I have wondered many times while sweating on a treadmill and having the ear plugs fall out, about how the same product can be so much easier to use with a wireless ear phone.

Call it product design or simple packaging, but the actual product presentation has an important task in today's marketing mix. Used well, it can do wonders for the brand in terms of establishing its values and enhancing its experience.

CHAPTER 17

RETHINKING YOUR SPORTS MARKETING MOVE (BASIS THE 2010 FIFA WORLD CUP SOUTH AFRICA)

The excitement of the World Cup has ended and the sound of the vuvuzelas is still ringing or perhaps droning in our ears every night after the finals had been played out. Any event like the FIFA World Cup is a huge marketing opportunity, and clearly, one relatively unexplored category that was discovered by the marketing fraternity after the Mexican Wave is the vuvuzela. Let's also take a look at what happened with the brands that were associated with the World Cup or with the players participating in the World Cup.

First off, think about the 2006 World Cup in Germany. One brand that perhaps had the least investment and still stood out significantly was Puma. As major sports brands built various associations with different players or teams, Puma adopted the underdog strategy. They did not sponsor the big teams or the big players but opted for unfancied teams with potential, and Italy happened to be one of those teams considered far behind Brazil, France, England and Germany. Italy, however, came good during the tournament, making it the World Champion and adding many layers of equity to the Puma brand in the process.

Four years have passed and consumer behaviour as well as the media consumption habits of consumers have undergone significant shifts and changes. All of these changes present huge opportunities for marketers, and for the first time, the World Cup was coming to the African continent, opening up a whole new wave of marketing possibilities.

Now consider what happened to some of the top-line brands that have built an association with this event across many years and of course invested significant sums of money in terms of sponsorships and commitment to the event. Adidas was one of the official sponsors of the World Cup, and as had happened during the previous World Cup in Germany, Adidas also had the incredible privilege of being the official soccer ball provider for this World Cup. Very few brands get an opportunity of obtaining official endorsement of such an unprecedented magnitude as Adidas had got with this opportunity. The official ball, most of the major teams wearing Adidas t-shirts, and an exotic-sounding sub-brand – the Jabulani. Adidas' Jabulani Ball, developed by the Loughborough University, with a unique texture intended to improve aerodynamics, should have become one of the most aspired sub-brands in the sporting world and should have created a new level of aspiration for the Adidas brand. Instead, the Jabulani ball became the subject of comments bordering on criticism from players and coaches about its directional and controlling abilities. What was to become the new standard in soccer balls became a subject of debate from the professionals, and became a lost opportunity for Adidas. Of course the fact that the winning team wore Adidas-branded t-shirts made up for this in many and more ways.

Consider another trendsetting brand Nike, and the opportunity it had to create some new rules of marketing during the FIFA World Cup. In terms of brand endorsement, brand associations and creative promotions, one would have expected Nike to score a lot of goals during this World Cup. And Nike did start its campaign in the most exciting way possible. Bringing in its star endorsers—Ribery, Ronaldo, Rooney and Robinho—Nike launched the extremely memorable and exciting campaign centred on the theme of "Write the Future." The campaign showed what success would translate into for these players with kids being named after Rooney or coins being issued in Robinho's image. But, in what can be termed as an absolute irony, all the stars featured in the Nike commercial failed during the tournament. Naturally, Nike built its media strategy around the games that these stars were featuring in. And it did not help to watch the Rooney commercial while England were being outplayed on all fronts by Germany, or in watching the Robinho commercial as Brazil was about to be knocked out by The Netherlands during the quarter finals.

Another FIFA World Cup sponsor, McDonald's, made the most of their sponsorship through a simple and relevant approach. The McDelivery logo kept flashing on the TV screen in Singapore when matches were being broadcast, reminding viewers to order in. And with many McDonald's outlets open 24 hours, or delivery service available till even 3 am, clearly McDonald's was playing in consumers' minds as they watched late night matches and sought snacks and munchies to keep the awake.

The key elements of sports marketing have been linked to event sponsorships, team sponsorships or individual sponsorships and then building a series of campaigns, promotions and product lines around these substantive investments. Perhaps the FIFA World Cup experience has created a series of new options and opportunities for brands to build the right associations. One option is for brands to align with "promising" teams that are "trying hard." Sports brands could have built very strong associations with some of the African teams like Ghana. And given the challenges that these countries face, they could have also added social marketing layers, donating sports equipment to schools or building stadiums and other infrastructure besides sponsoring the national team. And underdog teams that are trying harder have huge support amongst viewers across countries.

The other option is for brands to use the digitisation of media and media consumption to their advantage. Instead of planning a campaign in advance, it may be worth considering for brands to sponsor key players and then try a very unique approach. Whenever a player scores or does extremely well in a particular match, use that footage to create an ad overnight, which can run subsequently. Audiences would have enjoyed watching this player's performance and would have been reading about it. Watching a brand commercial featuring this winning footage would take the brand's association with the player and its overall equity to a new level altogether. With the technology available at present, being story-board ready and translating it into an actual commercial featuring the winning footage is now eminently possible.

Social network gaming is another huge opportunity for brands that associate themselves with mega sports events. Surprisingly, no major sportswear brands created "sponsored" games for Facebook or Iphones featuring the key players that they were sponsoring during the World Cup. And games are a terrific way to overcome the weaknesses of the teams or players in which brands have invested huge monies, either not living up to their expectations or even failing miserably. Again, think of a team like France or Italy, or players like Messi who never really delivered during this World Cup. Imagine a brand-sponsored game which goes live on Facebook or through an iPhone application where fans can replay a game which a team they were supporting had lost the previous night, and by using their own gaming skills, they can make the team win. Imagine if a game could have allowed Messi to score against Germany and make Argentina enter the semis virtually. Then the brand sponsoring Messi or Argentina could have converted a defeat into a huge marketing advantage and continued to create excitement and relevance for the fans of the team or the player that they were sponsoring.

Technology and the changes in media consumption habits are presenting massive opportunities to marketers to fundamentally recast the rules of sport marketing. Now let's wait for the major brands to rewrite this rule book and make our sporting experiences more exciting than they have ever been in the past. Let's blow some vuvuzelas in anticipation…

CHAPTER 18

INDIA'S INADVERTENT EXPORTS (2010)

India is targeting 15 percent growth in exports during the 2010–11 financial year despite a 4.7 percent decline in the previous year. This is an aggressive target given the economic crisis and the measly growth forecasts from the world's mature economies. As India pulls out all the stops to achieving the ambitious growth target, I'd like to reflect on some of my own experiences with India's cultural exports.

We all know that human capital has been India's greatest export over the years. Indians and their ways have become an integral part of the national fabric in various countries. With a population of more than one billion within the country and an estimated 30 million people of Indian origin in all corners of the world, the phenomenon of Indian ubiquity is expanding. Besides the well-established export of people and of technological prowess, there is now a growing number of inadvertent exports that have slipped out of India and taken unintended forms.

I stumbled on a lot of these inadvertent exports while living and interacting with people in Tokyo and in Hong Kong. For example, working abroad, I am frequently (and at times with a tinge of hesitation) asked the question, "Do you eat curry for all your meals?"

The notion of being perceived as someone that could down some grease-dominated concoction meal after meal always made me smile. Looking at the menus of "Indian" restaurants (which were often run by Bangladeshis) in Tokyo made me realise the cause of the confusion. The choices were almost uniformly heavy and there seemed to be a competition to see which dish was the greasiest. The thought that for the average Japanese (who visited these places only once in a while) this represented my regular daily nutritional intake made me laugh almost enough to burn off the grease that came embedded in this food.

It is great that after attaining the status of Britain's national dish, the concept of curry and tandoori has become as common as pizza and burgers across the globe. But the linkage of all Indian cuisine to these foods makes me think India should work harder to demonstrate the benefits of a conventional Indian diet. It needs to promote the potential of the basic Indian thali: roti, sabzi, dal and chawal.

We all know there is no one definition of an "Indian Diet," given that it is a confluence of many diets from different parts of country. However, clubbing it into a generic notion of "curry cuisine" is not just an oversimplification but is also ignoring the nutritional properties of an Indian diet.

Many a times, while having lunch with colleagues, people were surprised (after trying the items in my lunch box) that vegetables could be converted into something so pleasing to the palate. My lunch was a complete contrast from their notion of vegetables as some raw fibre which needed to be forcibly consumed to balance out the daily meat intake. Clearly, if done right (and with less grease), India has perhaps perfected the art of making vegetables tasty. Protein seekers the world over are just discovering the nutrient potency of lentils. Moong, Chana, Rajma, Toor and other forms, further morphed into dal, dalimbi and sambars, have been providing us with the requisite proteins despite our no-meat or low-meat diets.

Now imagine the export potential of books and diet programmes built around "The Indian Way of Cooking Vegetables" or "The Power of Cooked Indian Lentils" and the goodness of "Whole-Wheat Fluffy Chapattis." That's a long way from the greasy curries that have come to represent Indian cuisine for many. There are many opportunities to make money on promoting healthy Indian food, from cook books, to cooking classes to ready-to-eat meals to restaurants.

The potential of a balanced, nutrition-rich Indian diet of whole grains, properly cooked vegetables and nutritious pulses is huge in today's world where rearing livestock for consumption is being classified as one of the biggest degrading factors for the environment. Throw in concerns about red meat and processed meat, and consumption of real Indian cuisine could address the growing global desire for sustainable and balanced nutrition.

Another inadvertent export, yoga, has already gone global and become a mainstream sport. I am too often asked questions about my favourite yoga asana and whether I do hatha yoga or power yoga. When I reply that I am a mere treadmill tackler who does no yoga, there is considerable surprise. People assume that all Indians are yoga practitioners.

Another quirky fitness option that seems to be rapidly gaining global acceptance along with belly dancing and pole dancing is Bollywood dancing. When we used to watch Jeetendra and Sridevi doing their jig in the South Indian remakes that hit the Bollywood marquees in the late eighties, we would often comment that their dance steps were clearly inspired by the physical training routines done daily in Indian schools. Little did we realise that we were presaging the future. Imagine sipping a cocktail and being queried about your abilities to do Bollywood dancing.

There are many other traditional Indian dance and martial art forms that are waiting to be modernised and adapted into fitness forms. From Bollywood Bharat Natyam to Kollywood Kathak, our traditional dance forms can become effective workout routines. Traditional Indian martial arts and wrestling routines can also be globalised. Kalaripayattu can be as hip as Kung Fu and traditional Kushti as happening as Capoeira globally.

In Hong Kong there was a lot of buzz about a series of graphic novels called *Devashard*, which were inspired by the stories of our very own Mahabharat and have characters modelled on Karna and others. This made me think about the great global potential of Indian heroes. Perhaps these volatile economic times are ripe for the resurrection of Indian mythological super heroes and historical figures.

India's own version of the graphic novel, Amar Chitra Katha, also has the potential to speak to kids all over the world. The tried and tested format can be extended to DVDs and movies. Toddlers around the world can discover Baby Hanuman and his devotional prowess alongside the ever-expanding Baby Einstein collections on DVD shelves.

Stories of Lord Hanuman, the god of devotion who can move mountains with his faith; of Bheem, who has the strength of a thousand elephants; and of Arjun's sharp shooting are all yarns with immense appeal to adults the world over. We need these heroes, especially during these volatile economic times, when we are riding through a (perhaps) bottomed-out economic cycle and reaching for a spiritual high.

Besides conventional growth segments, India's exports still have a huge potential that can drive export growth rate well above the targeted 15 percent.

CHAPTER 19

SOCIAL NETWORKING – CONNECT WHERE IT MATTERS (2010)

As per new statistics, email is becoming marginalised! And this, despite the fact that people are spending more and more time on the internet. It's not because of an alternative messaging phenomenon that is rapidly emerging, nor is it due to a tectonic technology shift. People are surfing more and more, but where web-surfers spent most of their time emailing earlier, they now spend almost all their surfing time social networking. Despite its limitations and its quirks, social networking is rapidly becoming a part of our routine, integral to how we spend our day. And as this phenomenon refuses to abate, the marketing community is trying to figure out ways to harness this emerging medium effectively. Think of the nascent stages when the internet was slowly streaming into our collective consciousness. For marketers it meant still thinking of print ads but gloating over the fact that the ad had a www. address in some part of the ad. And slowly, besides having a website presence, the thinking evolved into having banner advertisements on select sites with links to the website. Yes, the web provided immense interactivity but the marketing imagination of interactivity meant having websites, bigger and more intrusive banners, and perhaps some contests on the websites. Internet phenomenon like blogging and search-engine-based surfing drove fundamental changes in consumers' surfing behaviour, while marketers spent their time investing in and trying to figure out the ROI on bigger banner ads. Similarly, the current marketing approach to social marketing seems to be centred on having Facebook tags around web pages that people can 'like' and 'share,' creating Facebook pages for brands and services, and then focusing effort on getting people to 'like' those pages. This is a fundamentally a restrictive approach and closes out a magnitude of options that social networking opens to marketers.

First off, social network sites can be evolved into terrific market research tools. An examination of the type of profiles that like *The Family Guy* Facebook pages or the Manchester United pages or even the Lindsay Lohan page will provide a lot of insight on how some of these vehicles cut through conventional demographic stereotypes. Also, lots of people take quizzes and answer contests on Facebook, sharing the results with their friends, who then go on to take these quizzes themselves. Brands, product concepts and marketing incubation ideas can be successfully seeded through this route for marketers to get results from engaged customers, for example, 'the best shampoo for your type of hair' quiz by any shampoo brand, or 'the best trainers for your style of running' by sports brands, creating social networking properties.

People send everything from virtual flowers to cooking tips to their friends. And loads of branded options can be created here for sending on a standalone basis or within game formats. For instance, manufacturers of organic products can brand the vegetables on Farmville.

Finally, social networking helps in identifying and targeting affinity groups like vegetarians, rugby lovers, beer enthusiasts or just plain reading buffs. It's time for brands to start their marketing plan with a social marketing strategy first and then evolve it to other media rather than the conventional other-way-around approach!

CHAPTER 20

THE ALL-IN-ONE BRAND PROPOSITION (2010)

Imagine, you set out to buy a computer. There are options in terms of the type of computer desktops, laptops and notepads you can choose. Once you zero in on a brand, you need to look for a processor or the chip that powers the brand you have chosen. Naturally, it should be a branded, new-generation chip. Next, you need to figure out whether the web camera and speaker options are part of the deal. You also need to load an operating system. And you are still not done because you have to decide on an appropriate anti-virus software. After going through this entire process, you probably have a computer that is ready to be plugged in and can connect to the internet.

From the consumer's point of view, the basic need is for a plug-and-play machine that loads internet sites, supports standard word processing and calculation formats, and importantly, does it all quickly.

There are a plethora of branded and non-branded options that exist within the various sub-segments, from the basic machine to the operating system, the powering chip to the anti-virus software. And brands such as Intel (for chips) and Symantec and Norton (for anti-virus software) have done a commendable job in establishing the benefits of their brands, making them critical components of the overall purchase. They have also done an excellent job in co-branding and partnering with hardware makers and electronics retailers to become an integral part of the overall solution.

Given the core customer need for a machine that works fast and can connect to the internet, is there an opportunity for brands to straddle various sub-categories and provide a complete solution to customers? Can a brand evolve from being strong in a sub-segment to becoming a total solutions brand that takes care of all or almost all customer needs, and provides a near holistic solution to a customer need with relevant benefits?

It is already happening to some extent. Think of the iconic Apple which makes its own core hardware and operating system. Add to that, Apple provides its own browser, and in many parts of the world, it also provides value-added benefits around graphics, music and animation. Apple has successfully embarked on a journey where a brand provides a holistic solution to a customer need and does it in style.

Retailers have embraced the concept of providing a complete solution. Furniture retailers advertise the availability of bedroom and living room sets, besides sofas and beds. Electronic brands also need to embark on a journey where they provide a complete package that includes guarantees, servicing options, and of course, prompt and reliable installation benefits. After all, think about the many instances when, after buying a top-end air conditioner, you have to wait several days for the installation personnel to arrive.

The bigger question is, can this concept of brands providing a complete solution to a customer need be extended to the fast-moving consumer goods category?

Well, it has already started happening. Consider the launch of Ariel detergent many years ago in India, when Surf and Nirma were ruling the roost. At that time, washing machines were not omnipresent, and the standard washing process in households entailed three stages – soaking the clothes in a detergent, washing them using a washing bar, followed by rinsing. Ariel was launched as a single-bucket wash concept, where all that was needed to complete one's washing was to soak the clothes in Ariel for some time and rinse them out.

High-end cosmetic brands have also been promoting skin solutions where an anti-ageing routine may comprise a face wash, a night cream and a sun screen. Of course, each of these products can meet a consumer's needs for sun protection or a dry skin solution on a standalone basis.

The men's shaving category is another example. Gillette has focused on providing a complete shaving solution that includes shaving cream, razors, blades and after-shaves. And the brand solution extends to Gillette's high-end products such as the Fusion range of shaving gels, razors, blades and after-shave protectors.

In the fast-moving consumer goods category that has been micro-segmented on many dimensions, toothpastes are available across myriad price points and consumer needs. From toothpastes for sensitive teeth, to herbal toothpastes, to stain-removing toothpastes, choices are abound.

Even in this crowded market place, Japan's number one dental care brand, Lion, provides a complete brand solution in Singapore. Lion's Systema brand has been positioned on the gum-care benefit but the brand communication does not restrict itself to a toothpaste that helps strengthen gums, but a holistic solution of a mouthwash, an inter-dental brush and an inter-dental brush gel, a radically different and integrated approach that not only provides opportunities for extending the brand within the realm of the core platform of improving gum health, but also sensitises consumers to the need for a different approach than simply changing one's toothpaste to maintain gum health.

For time-challenged customers, clearly, brands that provide an integrated solution to their needs will have a stronger significance. And for brands, the concept of a brand solution provides extension opportunities that will help them strengthen their relationship with their target segment.

CHAPTER 21

CARING FOR INDIA'S IGNORED GENERATION (2010)

Thanks to the demographics, India is viewed worldwide as a "young society." In Japan and Singapore, two developed societies where I have lived, there is increasing attention being paid to the other end of the spectrum: the elderly. As these societies age, they are rediscovering their respect for the elderly and the need to provide them with emotional, financial and physical support during their twilight years.

Unfortunately, we can't say the same about India. While India's economic growth trajectory keeps trending upward, the social aspects of this growth on the elderly merit a deeper understanding and perhaps some fundamental changes.

Let me elaborate a bit on my own personal experiences during a recent trip to my home – Mumbai.

Yes, property prices are rising in our neighbourhood. But many of these in-demand homes are now populated by elderly couples, widowed septuagenarians—if not octogenarians—battling diabetes, heart disease, the stress of managing their daily existence, all combined with a heavy dose of loneliness. Yet we seem to have become a society where it is widely accepted that children are supposed to be independent and that there is no longer a burden on the oldest children, as there is in Japan and Singapore, to look after their aging parents.

But let's look at that attitude from the mindset of this older generation. Eking out a typical middle-class life in the socialistic landscape of Nehru's India, and fired up by post-independence idealism, this generation devoted their entire lives to creating just one asset class: well-educated children ready to take on the world. This was their only retirement plan and their healthcare insurance provider for old age. Now, suddenly, this generation finds itself with little protection from the asset they invested their lifetimes in.

The social implications of this will play out in coming years. And if we acknowledge this phenomenon as today's reality, then the other issue that arises is – what sort of services and support systems exist that allow the elderly to live on their own?

This is also an opportunity for enterprises given that elderly services in India have meant little more than reserved seats on buses and trains and higher-yielding deposits from banks.

Here are some business options that need to rapidly evolve to enable today's urban elderly to live well:

- **Elder-friendly homes and furniture:** Homes in India need to be redesigned for the elderly to live alone and well. Right from furniture to bathrooms to fixtures, all need to be made elder-friendly. Alarm systems linked to co-operative societies or to emergency helplines need to be introduced.

- **Health insurance for the elderly, including insurance for pre-existing conditions:** Policies that provide coverage to the elderly despite pre-existing health conditions need to be introduced. This is not just restricted to creating policies but managing the whole process of policy issuance and of claims-processing in an elder-friendly manner.

- **Money management for the elderly:** This does not just mean bank deposits. Banks have to change their orientation to provide elder-friendly branches, branch assistants who can take care of all banking transactions that the elderly need, and of course, financial advice to help the elderly manage their meagre savings.

- **Elder-caregivers:** Many of the elderly suffer from chronic conditions like diabetes in India and need to be administered daily doses of insulin and oral medications. Highly trained, full-time and part-time elder-caregivers are critical.
- **Domestic support for the elderly:** This includes providing household workers, cooks and drivers for the elderly to manage their homes, to get hot, nutritious food; and of course, to get mobility in today's crammed urban areas where there is place to walk and precious little space to park.
- **Counselling services:** Loneliness and chronic diseases take their toll on the mental wellbeing of the elderly. Accessible elderly counselling services is another glaring gap that needs to be addressed.
- **Recreational areas:** Parks and walking spaces have never been a priority in our urban development. These now need to be embedded at least for new developments to ensure that the elderly have access to some form of recreation and exercise.
- **Volunteerism backed by adequate incentives:** India's youth needs to engage more in supporting their elders. Companies need to provide leave and other relevant incentives to get staff members to engage in volunteerism to provide emotional and other support to the elderly.
- **Reemployment opportunities:** Many of the lonely elderly may still be able to work and contribute post retirement. Reemployment centres that can create opportunities with limited working hours and less physical and mental stress could be created.

It's time to create support systems that light up the twilight years for the Independence generation that has now become the ignored generation. Naturally, this is a huge business opportunity also.

CHAPTER 22

HOW INDIA CAN HELP NRIS INVEST (2011)

India is officially top in cricket. It also has almost the fastest-growing major economy in the world and has been projected by some to exceed China's growth in the years to come. And recently, it came out number one in remittances, according to the World Bank.

Indians remitted $52 billion to India in 2010, closely followed by China at $51 billion, and trailed significantly by Mexico which received $22 billion from its overseas population.

The report estimates that worldwide remittance flows total $440 billion, so overseas Indians account for about 12 percent. With Indians across social strata actively seeking opportunities abroad, coupled with their willingness to travel anywhere from Poland to Paraguay, remittances home will surely increase.

Also enabling these flows is the widespread presence of institutions like banks and remittance providers that allow the money earned by Indians abroad to be sent to Indians in rural areas who may not even have a bank account.

However, it is important to consider certain areas that need attention to ensure that the flows remain strong, and that the Non-Resident Indian population gets the assurances it needs to keep sending money back home.

From my own experience, besides sending money for parents and dependents, one of the biggest reasons NRIs seek to send money to India is to build or keep a home. For emotional reasons and family ties, there will always be NRIs willing to invest in their hometowns in India. But what are they up against?

First, housing finance companies and mortgage-issuing banks do everything from housing exhibitions at overseas locations to instant loan approvals, but largely confine their activities to property purchase opportunities in big metros. Given the considerable population that is from semi-urban and rural areas, there are very few ways an NRI can invest in a property in, say, Meerut or Mangalore while sitting in a foreign country.

Second, the construction sector is totally disorganised, so finding the right builder is an insurmountable challenge. Even if one finds a reputable builder, local documentation requirements are a nightmare to manage remotely and require a host of in-person visits. The property registration formalities even in a thriving, wannabe global metro like Mumbai are mind boggling to say the least.

Third, think about what NRIs are up against if they want to rent the property. The smaller inconveniences like managing utility and tax payments on a property are another burden.

Without the support system of an extended Indian family within India, very little of this can be managed by NRIs.

What are we up against in terms of competing for NRI dollars?

Property developers from across the world regularly advertise property in prime global hubs like Hong Kong, offering not only upscale properties but a host of value-added benefits that include completing all the purchase formalities and offering mortgages as well as providing additional services like managing all utility and tax payments and arranging rentals. Some even arrange for rental payments to be remitted overseas.

In India, it would seem a major opportunity for enterprising developers to provide turnkey property services that take care of documentation, registration, utility payments and tax payments. This can also be extended further into providing rental clients and managing rent collection and rent remittances.

Another critical gap in our NRI proposition is linked to investments and insurance. After NRIs were targeted through the successful India Millennium Bonds in 2000, there have been very few investment vehicles that have evolved specifically for NRIs.

The opportunity can play out in many forms from unique financial instruments that only NRIs can invest in to sector specific funds created for NRIs. Just as an example, funds and bonds which allow NRIs to invest in India's infrastructure or education development could be a huge opportunity.

The start that banks and mortgage companies have made is only the beginning. A few simple measures can go a long way towards making India the preferred destination for parking NRI savings.

At present, the story is one of little progress. Take the case of NRI voting rights. That has finally come through after years of noise from the NRI community. But it is another case of the right step being taken without due consideration of how it might work. As it stands, it requires NRIs to be there in person IN INDIA to vote; it does not allow them to exercise their voting rights through embassies or absentee ballots as other countries do.

CHAPTER 23

THE BUILDING BLOCKS OF OUTDOOR MEDIA (2011)

Marketers continue to wade through the challenges posed by the blurring lines between online and offline media and its ever-changing form. Television is all about clutter and wading through massive choices to find a programme that appeals, or making a choice to ignore the television set altogether and simply to watch content online or through DVDs at one's own pace. Similarly for print, consumers can choose to stick with newspapers and magazines, or access the same content through e-readers or simply switch to online consumption. There is, however, one area which still represents a huge opportunity for marketers to drive home uncluttered awareness and even go beyond awareness to establish product benefits and brand values. In addition, this option can also be used to build levels of interactivity and opportunities to engage with the brand in exciting ways. That option is outdoors. Consumers like to settle into a bus, train or taxi and take a look around what they are driving past, even when they are talking on the phone or playing on their mobile phones. Similarly, receptivity to marketing messages is higher when consumers are simply walking or waiting at trains and bus stations. There are, of course, a few building blocks to harnessing this medium effectively for maximum impact.

The first building block is **consistency**. Ever since its launch, H&M has taken a set of billboards in Hong Kong, and continues to refresh their messaging. Sticking to one location for a committed period significantly enhances awareness. The messaging format has also been kept homogeneous and standard around three elements, including attractive models with even more attractive clothes, a clear mention of the price – making sure that value registers as a integral element of the brand, and ongoing new collections to coincide with seasons or designers collaborating with H&M.

The second building block is **compatibility to the consumer's consumption need**. Beer brands like Carlsberg and Tiger Beer in Singapore are splattered all over buses. After a hard day's work and the perennial heat and humidity of Singapore, a cold beer seems like the best thing in the world during the evening commute home.

The third building block is **captivating messaging** in terms of form and content. Is the messaging bringing out the brand values in a striking and catchy manner? Can the outdoor message be something that serves as a standalone and memorable means of brand communication? On a recent trip to India, I noticed a unique way of messaging in an outdoor campaign for Gatorade. A dummy climber trying to climb through a large rope in the billboard not only had very high noticeability, but even brought out the sports nutrition benefit of the brand in a very clear manner.

The last emerging building block is **connectivity**. Think about the proliferation of 3G and smart phones that allow people to get online in a flash. Starting in Japan, the QR code technology allows interested users to go straight to the brand's website through a click of the phone's camera. It allows marketers to use outdoor as a medium to kindle interest and lead interested prospects straight to their websites with detailed brand benefits, more detailed visual advertising messages and the opportunity for immediate purchase. Now is the time to embed connectivity in all outdoor campaigns, as QR codes continue to evolve to become even more interactive and customer friendly.

CHAPTER 24

BEYOND VISUAL APPEAL – THE TOUGHER ELEMENTS OF AN AD CAMPAIGN (2016)

I recently came across the ads done by the state of Rajasthan with some incredible themes, a lovely story line, beautiful visuals and a huge repeat value. A campaign that excites, intrigues and merits watching again and again. Kudos to the agency that has developed this campaign and created something remarkably memorable and worth watching again.

However this campaign also summarises the challenge that India's domestic or international tourism sector faces. India gets only a fraction of the tourists that smaller countries or city states like Hong Kong, Singapore or Thailand receive. India's ranking in terms of tourism arrivals is a lowly 41st.

Let us examine the Rajasthan Tourism campaign to understand more in terms of what ails India's tourism sector. The solution to addressing any problem is to create a memorable campaign that is creative, has huge repeat value, and makes one feel like packing one's bags and heading there. But everything begins and ends with just one element – a campaign. There is no multipronged strategy unveiled to drive tourism into the state. The elements of a holistic plan are either never created, and if they are, then they are never made public.

Take this same Rajasthan Tourism campaign. Besides a brilliant advertising concept that is extremely well executed, there should have been at least the following strategic actions that should have been announced:

1) Increase in inbound flights to key tourism linked destinations of Rajasthan from standard and from budget fare airlines. Similarly increase in trains and luxury buses to bring tourists spanning across income strata. You see a beautiful location in an ad, and then discover that to go there one has to take one flight, one bus and a car ride, all of which are at inconvenient times. This does not allow one to pack one's bags and go there immediately. Developing convenient access to these wonderful locations has to be done prior to launching a campaign, and should be announced along with the campaign for those interested to use.

2) Upgradation and addition of hotel rooms in the key tourism destinations. It is not uncommon to face the following constraints once one has made up their mind on a destination – a few luxury hotels that are pre-booked during holiday season, and if a room is available then it is going for a rate which is five times the rate of a good hotel in Singapore. Another scenario is where you set your heart on a place, then look up the hotels and you find that there is only one circuit house available for accommodation there, built during the British era, that is now booked for Babus, MLAs and their ilk for the next three months.

3) Segment approach in terms of additional facilities for the tourist profiles sought. People do not come to just see monuments. People come on leisure. For upper-end tourists, this may mean golf courses to tee off in addition to luxury hotels. For families, it could mean amusement parks built around historic and cultural themes to visit in addition to the monuments. For the active tourist, it means jogging tracks and outdoor/indoor fitness activities. These need to be planned, built and provided before the launch of any campaign.

4) Tourist friendly initiatives – do the monuments and the living areas around them have enough of the following: ATMs for cash withdrawal, licensed and reliable forex exchange houses to

convert foreign currency to rupees, enough credit card-accepting outlets, inspected and certified hygienic restaurants across price points, ample pure drinking water, public sanitation in terms of clean toilets and certified knowledgeable tourist guides. Also, medical facilities and even sufficient power. Sitting in a rundown hotel near a beautiful monument with power outages and no hot water does not make a dream destination for anyone.

5) The most important and the most negative aspect of tourism in India is security. What are the concrete measures taken to enhance security for local and international tourists. The biggest fear anyone has of visiting any place in India today is lack of security. From private security to armed guards to amiable English-speaking cops, who tourists can find easily, are basics to make anyone feel like visiting a place.

6) Making visas accessible and easier. How have the visa processes been modified to make visas easier, faster and cheaper?

7) A real target. No campaign is complete without a real target in terms of the number of tourists to be attracted and a clear increase in targeted revenues.

I write this because on one side I am seeing this lovely campaign which a lot of people are admiring and sharing on media. On another side, I am seeing a tourism development plan mentioned in another country that is a revelation. It has concrete measures on development of golf resorts, a cultural event, a half marathon event, an amusement park, clear addition of rooms and flights, all articulated. There is no mention of a campaign. Because an advertising campaign is the tail and perhaps a shining tail of a tourism enhancement initiative, it is not the beginning and the end of that drive as practised by tourism boards in India.

CHAPTER 25

FACTORING IN FIRST IMPRESSIONS TO CREATE BRAND LOYALTY (2016)

Many years ago, stepping into teenage from boyhood, I acquired this burning desire for a branded pair of jeans. At that time in India, there was only one option of local branded jeans available – FUs. Being the only option for a large population that was entering the "jeans phase" of their lives, the brand had a huge advantage going for it. Armed with some pocket money, I entered their branded store. Immediately a salesperson said, "Each pair of jeans here is over rupees 400." Shocked, I ran out to Elco Arcade nearby, where a friendly tailor offered tea while taking measurements, and provided a pair at one third the cost. That was my first and only interaction with the FUs brand.

This brings me to a critical aspect that all marketers and brand managers need to manage in today's world that is rapidly changing and evolving. The first impression and interaction with the brand, I call it the First Impression Factor in the marketing mix. An aspect that needs huge attention and serious over management

Let us start with the airlines industry. An airline promises chauffeur drops in the country you land in. That would be a sterling benefit for business travellers. Landing at a new airport, I head out, assured that my ride is waiting, only to find that the queue to avail of this chauffeur drop is bigger than the queue for normal taxis. Once I got into the car, the driver immediately asked me if I knew the way to my hotel. Sheepishly he says he is new there and does not quite know his way around. He finally calls up a few people to get directions and takes an additional hour to get me through. Throughout the ride, I kept asking questions to myself on why the driver could not be provided with a GPS, why he could not be briefed in advance on traveller destinations and be given route maps.

Another area is hotels. Tired and drained, you enter a reputed hotel for your business trip and are greeted with a massive queue at check-in. During check-in you are informed about the fact that a late check-out is not possible as – "We are fully booked."

Jet lagged and bedraggled, you make it into your room. The funny key contraption given to you does not work. You are now faced with the prospect of going down fourteen floors to get another set of keys. At the reception they ask if you kept your keys with your mobile phone, because the key management programme stops working if you did. Finally, you make it to your room and you cannot find where the lights are. Searching for lights in an unknown room at 4 AM in the morning does not make for a favourable first impression. A brand that has emerged recently and has mastered this First Impression Factor is The Pullman chain. In my experience, they always get it right on the First Impression Factor front across geographies, thereby ensuring repeat business from business travellers across the globe.

Even as mobile applications become an integral part of our lives, the First Impression Factor becomes even more salient. I recently downloaded Entertainment Arts' FIFA 2015 app and opened it. For the next 10 minutes I got the message – *Our servers are experiencing heavy traffic, we are working on it.* App deleted. The Indian app-ecommerce world is rife with horror stories of first-time-user experiences on food delivery and grocery delivery applications. Over promising and no delivery, not just under delivering. This is a complete contrast to Amazon where the entire First Impression Factor for a new to Amazon user is geared towards converting this "just looking" visitor into a frequent site visitor and a loyal shopper.

Imagine when you receive your credit card with great anticipation. Farhad Irani, a pioneer of the credit cards category in India, actually highlighted the importance of these card delivery packs, and rechristened them 'Welcome Packs' with three mandatory I's – Informative, Interactive and Intuitive. Contrast that with 'Delivery Packs' of today, stuffed with all kinds of irrelevant terms where a customer may end up tearing the actual card itself, which is lost in all the junk content.

Singapore is a shining example of getting the First Impression Factor right. You arrive at a world class airport where even the cleanliness of toilets can be given a service rating and water can be drunk from any tap. And then you can get from this airport to the heart of the city in just twenty minutes. All thanks to GVK's efforts, there is a world class airport in Mumbai, where immigration forms are not required. But even GVK can do nothing about the 'Customs Declaration Form' that one has to fill only after arriving. No escape from some form of form filling!

As Malcolm Gladwell put it – "Our first impressions are generated by our experiences and our environment, which means that we can change our first impressions…by changing the experiences that comprise those impressions." It is time for marketers to incorporate the First Impression Factor in their marketing mix to create brand loyalty and preference.

CHAPTER 26

THE LEFT-OUT SEGMENT (2016)

I used to love drawing in class. My sketches and illustrations came out pretty well. But in school, during those days, art was never a standalone subject. It was always art and craft. And craft was one area where I simply could not cope, forget excel. Making peacocks out of paper, cutting sheets into elephants – fun and simple activities that I simply could not get right. Needless to add, my grades always suffered because my art was okay but my craft was always challenged.

School was also about filling supplements to answer sheets as quickly as I could, competing with other students. And this was another area where I just could not get things done quickly. Increasingly, I acquired the label of a "slow writer." No matter how hard I studied for exams, my friends and fellow students knew that given my pace of writing, I would never be able to put all my thoughts on paper. So I was not competition, and the aspiring first-rankers never needed to worry about what I would answer and submit because it was not as copious in quantity as what they submitted.

And then there was the label of 'Master Non-Mechanical.' I was an absolute disaster at using any tools. Many times, when Mom needed help with using a can opener or a peeler, it was a clear rule that asking me to help would result in the can getting badly punched but never opened. And then, my sister would take the can opener, use it as if it was the simplest thing to use in the world, and open the can with a flourish and a swish. I started living with this realisation that I was perhaps not meant to do any scissor-wielding craft, and should not be doing anything mechanical given my complete lack of skills in that aspect.

Designed for People Like Me

Then many years later, I walked into a lovely pen store of a German brand called Lamy. Lamy fountain pens are distinctive in design with a unique look combined with all the greatness of German engineering. The store had also thoughtfully laid out a trial section for store visitors to try out the various pens and just play around a bit. A bold, brown fountain pen struck my eye. Being a collector of fountain pens in this era of keyboard and styluses, I picked it up and started scribbling on the sheet of paper. It was either my scribble or my efforts, I do not know what happened, but I suddenly seemed to have caught the attention of the store attendant. She came and observed my attempt. Then looked at me and said, "Sir, we have a special pen nib designed for people like you." What exactly was specially designed for a common person like me? Doubting that she was simply trying to sell some expensive piece to me, I said I am not interested and kept up my attempt at scribbling. Then she looked at me again and said, "Sir, we have a specially-designed nib for left-handed people." Naturally, I happily purchased the nib and pen, which I have been using since then. And I realised that I was also part of a unique, underserved and growing segment.

Left-handed people are estimated to be about 10 percent of the world's population. Extrapolating that statistic to one billion Indians, one can estimate that there should be 100 million Indians who are left-handed across all age groups. And marketers seem to have made little of the unique needs and attitudes of this segment.

First off, there is a massive gap in terms of functional products customised for use by left-handed people. Like the Lamy Nib, there is only one example of a franchise called Lefty's the Left Handed Store which exists in a few countries. I had the privilege of visiting one in San Francisco and it was a revelation in terms of unmet needs.

There were scissors and pencils specially designed for left-handed people. Using one of these made me realise that I was not bad at craft after all. I just did not have the "right tools and equipment," as they say. While the focus at the Lefty's store is largely on day-to-day, utilitarian items, seeing these actually in a store, along with the Lamy experience, made me realise the massive gap that exists in today's marketplace in terms of products designed and available for a significant 10 percent of the world's population.

Let's start with the mobility category for instance. Most places in the world have people driving on the right side of the road and the steering wheel of the car is on the left side. This means that the gears which need as much controlling as the steering wheel are always on the right side of the driver. Great for a right-handed driver and not so great for a left-handed driver. Take motorcycles for instance: the accelerator needs to be used the most and it is always on the right side, with the brake on the left side. For a left-handed person, to drive his mobike with ease, it should be the other way round.

Move on to the ubiquitous mobile phones. Steve Jobs, while he claimed to be left-handed, was actually more right-handed if the design of the iPhone is anything to go by. The on/off switch, one of the most important buttons on the iPhone is on the top right hand corner. Great for right-handed people and not so much for left-handers. Hence, I prefer to simply silence my phone on the left side than try to switch it off.

Take all those ubiquitous apps that all of us spend most of our day on. If there is a car-racing app, then the steering wheel is always on the right side, making it very difficult for a left hander to excel at the game.

Get down to shirts and belts. Almost all shirts have buttons on the right side. Doing their buttons is always easier for right-handers while left-handers can easily mess that up. There can be a whole category of garments designed and created for left-handers. In fact, I recall that many years ago, Louis Philippe had launched shirts in India where their famous crest actually appeared on the left cuff. This was a great concept that was killed before it went mainstream, because I was one of the eager buyers who went store to store, only to be informed that supplies of that particular type of shirt had stopped, which brings one to the non-functional aspect and the linked marketing potential of being left-handed.

Customise, Customise!

From apparel to accessories to footwear, there is a whole range of products that can be customised in terms of functionality for left-handed people and can also display their uniqueness in some way. After all, who would not like to display that they are in the same league as Michelangelo, Tom Cruise, Robert De Niro, Napoleon, Julius Caesar, and our very own Amitabh Bachchan, to name a few.

Now here is a potential global franchise that needs some left-brain thinking to develop across the world. Brands such as the Lefty Store and Lamy are just scratching at the fingertip of this left hand at present.

CHAPTER 27

ADDING THE "VIABILITY" PERSPECTIVE TO THE BUSINESS OF FINANCIAL INCLUSION

India has in theory created what is envisaged to be a major financial inclusion driver in the form of 'payments banks,' a whole new vehicle aiming to establish a new paradigm of financial inclusion.

The basic elements are well covered in the RBI guidelines issued including deposit-taking of up to Rs. 10,000 per account, remittances, selling of products such as insurance, issue of debit cards and no lending. There is a rider that payments banks cannot lend or issue credit cards.

Overall, the initiative has all the key components. Yet, while eleven licences were issued, there has been a surprising turn where three entities granted these licences – Cholamandalam, IDFC Bank-Telenor-Sun Pharma combined and Tech Mahindra have already pulled out. That is a near 20 percent drop-off rate from institutions which have already created business plans around this initiative even before it began. Naturally, the key consideration driving this decision would be financial viability, and cost to serve such a low-revenue generating segment.

Consider these for mainstreaming the whole financial inclusion initiative:

Rewiring the Source: Payments banks aim to include unbanked small businesses, low-income households and the migrant labour force. The current model envisages creating a distribution infrastructure, both physical and virtual, where, say, a migrant worker or a labourer can walk into and open a deposit account.

Now consider the source of funds for the labourers. They get paid almost entirely in cash with no record of when the payment was made and no clear audit trail in most cases, given that most businesses employing them want to save on taxes.

Many years ago, markets such as the UAE also had a similar challenge where a labour force was paid entirely in cash and there was no record, resulting in issues of insufficient payments against contracts and lack of timely payments.

The solution: It is mandated that in the UAE, all migrant workers get their payments not through cash but through a prepaid card where the amount is credited, just the way payroll is processed for most salaried workers. These prepaid cards provide cash withdrawal through connected ATM networks either free or at a very nominal cost that is also added to the payout to ensure the worker does not suffer any loss of pay.

What if small industries are mandated to make a payment through a prepaid Rupay card, India's own payment network, where the cost per transaction both to the issuer (the payments bank issuing the card) and to the acquiring bank (the ATM owner) is minimal? There is also the requirement of a tax concession where the entity making payments through such means will not only be not taxed but will get significant concessions. Imagine a small factory owner now paying his workers, not through cash, but through a prepaid card owing to not just regulation but also a huge tax advantage.

The second challenge of financial inclusion is financial knowledge, and experience is the best teacher. Once unbanked customers start using their own prepaid cards, the knowledge they acquire on managing their cash and linked saving options also increases.

While the RBI has mandated 25 percent physical presence in unbanked/ rural areas, and physical distribution points tend to be expensive, this option of prepaid cards also allows for using concepts such as mobile ATMs with low capex. Saving plans and insurance sales can also be provided through these mobile ATMs.

Broadbasing Distribution: Many of the unbanked prospects work for small industries such as grocery stores. One can safely estimate that 99 percent of the transactions, if not more, at these stores happen in cash. Today, there is an extremely versatile cashless solution available in the form of Card Acceptance Point of Sale (PoS) machines which can be procured for less than $100. These machines can accept all cards, including prepaid cards, and it does not end at that. They can also be programmed to provide cash advances on these cards. So a worker employed in a grocery store can get his salary on a prepaid card, buy groceries for his own consumption using it and can also withdraw cash right at the store from the PoS machine.

For this, it is critical to make all payments banks, default payment card acquirers at least for India's home-grown payment network Rupay. This will allow payments banks to create distribution points at low cost using devices like the credit card accepting PoS machines.

Once there is sufficient traction on both prepaid cards and acceptance points that double up as cash withdrawal points, there is a whole new play that comes into effect. Many of these customers can now get a credit score depending on their salary credits and usage, getting access to lending. And payments banks can refer these cases to lenders with full information, opening up a whole new source of fee revenue for them, where lenders pay for these references without the banks taking any risks.

Finally, these consumers also have spending needs for which they get little or no loyalty. Payments banks can now create loyalty and discount programmes tailored to everything this consumer base uses, from prepaid mobile cards to cooking oil. The loyalty points can also go into special savings programmes, such as special education funds for children, with higher-than-market returns.

Microfinance emerged from Bangladesh and the unique MPESA money transfer service emerged from Kenya. India's payments banks can set global benchmarks for pioneering the mainstreaming of low-cost financial inclusion and more.

CHAPTER 28

THROWBACK TO TURNTABLES – HOW NOSTALGIA CAN WORK WONDERS FOR THE MARKETING MIX (2016)

Guess what was the fastest-growing audio product category at Amazon during the end of the holiday season in 2015? If one were to ask me, my spontaneous response would be a Bluetooth speaker. After all, every home wants one now. If probed further, I would have ventured into the ubiquitous wireless headphone. So I actually looked up the number one product and it was neither of these. It was a product that went out of our frame of reference, perhaps in the seventies…a product that we largely associated with black-and-white photographs and an object in the homes of our grandfathers and great-grandfathers. Amazingly, the top-selling audio product on Amazon was a Jensen JTA 3 speed-stereo turntable.

The fact that a long-forgotten relic of the past had streamed or rather played its way back into our consciousness struck me sometime last year when a very close friend invited me to dinner. His idea of a perfect evening with friends was, of course, good food and wine, but also an evening spent listening to records. Records or vinyls, as they are called in the west. One did not even know that they existed. And the record collection that he was building included not just songs but even a dialogue record of *Sholay*. He used to make regular trips to a shop at Chandni Chowk in Delhi from Dubai, where we lived then, to search for and purchase old records. When I asked him why he was investing in vinyl and in changing records to play music in this era of unlimited songs on a hard drive or through a streaming service, he said it simply sounded better. And like him, millions of people with huge music collections and audio equipment in MP3 and other such formats are rediscovering the bygone magic of records and the turntable.

Marketing Mix

Nostalgia and heritage are two elements in a marketing mix that can revivify and revitalise categories rather than make them fade away. And just as it is happening with the revival of turntables, there have been brands that have a rich heritage, and have used it to not just resurrect their category but make it even more relevant to generations that have never experienced it but only know about it. One great example of constantly reinvigorating a past category is the Adidas Stan Smith Originals series. Launched as a tennis shoe in 1973, the brand is still going strong. It has evolved from a tennis shoe to a sneaker to a customisable sneaker. It was reintroduced in 2014 with strong modern day features such as customisations and partnerships with new-age designers and with contemporary singers. Singer Pharrell Williams who appeals to a totally different generation than the one which grew up wearing the original Stan Smiths, was roped in to create his own line of hand-painted Stan Smiths which was a sell-out in 2015. The series continues to grow and to appeal to a whole new generation that was not even born when it was first launched.

Take Converse All Star, another brand founded in 1917 that had its best period between the 1940s and 1960s. With the entry of Nike, Reebok and Adidas in the 1970s, the brand had lost its relevance to both athletics and basketball. Even in India, the white tennis shoe or the so-called "canvas" shoe, our equivalent of Converse, gave way to sneakers from Reebok and Nike. The brand has successfully resurrected itself in recent times with Nike's astute marketing prowess and has extended its relevance not just to the generation that was used to wearing it while growing up, but to today's youngsters as a shoe that makes a fashion statement. It is a billion-dollar-plus brand in today's rapidly changed world.

Heritage clearly has an enduring appeal and can easily be resurrected and contemporised. And the same applies to this emerging but long-forgotten category of turntables. The appeal of this category need not be restricted to a generation craving a bygone era and immersed in nostalgia. It can actually be made relevant to an entire new generation. Record companies are already doing this by releasing new albums, not just on iTunes but also on turntables.

Technology has also evolved to make today's records clearer and turntables much more sophisticated compared to the screechy sound coming from an easy-to-bend e-pin during the seventies.

Waiting for Rebirth

Iconic but forgotten Indian brands are waiting to be reborn. Recently in Delhi, Keventers Milkshakes, bestsellers of the '60s and '70s have been relaunched. And social media is abuzz with people born during that period introducing this drink to their children born in the 21st century. And perhaps, the Murphy Radio will return with a 21st century baby as its mascot and with full FM functionality. After all, despite The Buggles singing it loud in 1979, video never really killed the radio star. Radio just returned as mainstream FM.

Marketers can rejoice at this whole new social phenomenon that has the power to revive and revitalise and revamp a forgotten category. Meanwhile I am discovering the joy of rediscovering *Sholay* just through its dialogues. And the tables have turned back again for turntables.

CHAPTER 29

ROAD SAFETY GEAR – AN UNTAPPED ROUTE (2016)

There is little hope for India's road infrastructure. Numerous discussions, debates and plans have emerged every year, and yet the story of battered roads, potholes and lack of roads continues.

As per published statistics, Indian roads are death traps with nearly 16 deaths every hour. And the crumbling infrastructure, combined with ever-increasing vehicles and traffic collisions, makes any kind of journey on Indian roads a hazard. India is one of the countries at the bottom in terms of WHO's Road Safety Report with two-lakh-plus reported deaths, and who knows how many are unreported.

The fact that road conditions have a slim chance of improving in the next few years is a reality. The increasing population of vehicles is another certainty. Take the two-wheeler market in India. Around 16 million two-wheelers are estimated to have been sold during 2014–15 in India, adding to 15 million sold in 2013–14, and another 13.7 million during 2012–13. Two-wheelers continue to be the most popular vehicle category in India and include scooters, motorbikes and mopeds. And no surprises that amongst all vehicles, two-wheelers account for the largest number of deaths and injuries.

Safety, a Neglected Opportunity

With road conditions not improving, the extent of paved surfaces staying the same and with two-wheelers piling up on the roads, one of the most under-leveraged categories in India is the entire two-wheeler safety category.

First, let us start with the good old helmet. In terms of market evolution, one would expect the top two-wheeler manufacturers to actually branch out into branded helmets – a Bajaj helmet with a Bajaj scooter and a Hero helmet with a Hero motorbike. However, most of the popular brands are ones such as Studds, Vega and Steelbird. While being a critical part of a two-wheeler, mainline helmet brands do not have the same level of awareness and saliency as the two-wheeler brands or even some of the lubricant brands that have made a huge effort in establishing their brand and its benefits. Surprisingly, for a market potential of 14 million new vehicles and a huge number of second-hand two-wheeler sales, the extent of branding and marketing done by the current helmet brands is way below potential.

Then comes the category-wise evolution. First is a linkage to vehicle type. So, ideally, a helmet designed for a scooter should be different from one designed for a moped. And the helmets designed for motorbikes need to be differentiated on the basis of a basic mobike versus a powerful mobike versus a high-performance biking enthusiast's HOG. While accessories including helmets are a huge contributor to the revenues of cult brands such as Harley Davidson and Ducati, there is also room for the mass manufacturers to link this protective gear to their core brands, which lies untapped today.

How about Stylish Helmets?

Another category evolution opportunity is gender-based. Many bikes, such as Kinetic Honda and TVS Scooty, target youngsters or young women who want a taste of freedom. Specially-designed safety helmets for these types of bikes and their users are another untapped opportunity.

Additionally, while there have been many public awareness campaigns on the safety aspect of helmets, and even on regulation making helmets mandatory in some cases, there has been little marketing and branding activity to make helmets desirable. Creating helmet designs, colours and styles that reflect the driver's personality is yet another unexploited opportunity, not to forget helmet forms and styles to endure weather conditions, ranging from summer to heavy rains to winter and snow. Nobody has tried to move this category from a regulation-driven utility to an extension of one's personality or something with flash value and attitude.

Besides the lack of development in helmets, a bigger issue is the lack of evolution of the entire two-wheeler personal safety equipment category itself. Take India's favourite passion – the game of cricket. At one time there were only gloves and pads. Then came Sunil Gavaskar with his forearm guard and skull cap. Now players have guards for all sensitive body parts and more to face the 100-km-and-more-per-hour swing.

Meanwhile, the entire fast-growing category of two-wheelers with millions of first-time users is saddled with just one piece of safety equipment – a helmet. This is where category evolution is seriously required. Imagine a jacket or even an inner vest that provides spine protection, one of the most vulnerable areas during any collision, and the cause of so many disabilities besides death. If well-designed, spine-protecting equipment can become a fashion statement for many riders.

Knees are another highly vulnerable area for two-wheeler riders. Knee-protection devices can range from basic pads to trousers to colourful wraparounds on the knees that can, again, become chic and trendy with colours, designs, and customisation.

Now, one comes to the other critical form of urban transport that has had zero evolution in terms of safety measures. The humble, revered, and much-exported autorickshaw. I know of a dialysis patient whose driver did not turn up one morning. She took an auto to get to the hospital for her dialysis session. Thanks to the lack of signals and urban planning, the auto driver tried to take a quick turn into the hospital gate to avoid a speeding car coming at him, and the rickshaw overturned. The patient ended up injuring her hand on which the dialysis procedure is done and had to spend a week in hospital. While millions and more passengers prefer to use autos for their urban transportation needs in our traffic-choked cities, there is not a single passenger-safety instrument that has been created for safe travelling in autos.

When you get on a ride in an amusement park, especially on roller-coasters, they have a safety harness that is affixed to the seat and wraps around one's shoulders as protection to prevent you from getting hurled around or falling out. The same concept can be adapted for autos so the three people sitting do not get hurled around when the auto tries to speed, do not get back problems when the auto navigates massive potholes, and do not get badly injured and thrown out when an auto overturns.

Seatbelts, the Clincher

And finally, we come to our good old hatchbacks, the staple of most Indians as a means of transport. As affordability, ambition and accessible credit drive the growth of cars, one of the biggest safety issues stands out. Unlike sophisticated, high-end Mercedes cars, the affordable hatchbacks do not come with air bags that self-activate in the event of a collision. So, the only safety mechanism that exists is the humble seat belt. And while steering wheels have evolved into power steering, and brakes have become more sensitive, the seat belt continues to be archaic and perhaps the most difficult mechanism to operate in a car.

There can be so many ways to manage the whole 'belting up' experience in a car than the current entangled belts that can cause one a backache while they are trying to pull them from wherever these things are hidden. Moreover, they are extremely difficult to adjust for rapidly expanding Indian bellies and are a task to strap on. A car with simple, easy-to-put-on seat belts can by itself become a phenomenon due to its exceptional safety features. Let us leave that to the kaizen masters at Suzuki to figure out. Perhaps auto-activation and de-activation with sensor-based self-adjusting straps is the solution waiting to emerge.

Poor road infrastructure and potholes will continue to be a reality. Cars, two-wheelers and autos as a segment will continue to grow and crowd these creaky and broken-down roads. But the evolution of the mobility safety category, which is a huge opportunity for marketers, can actually help bring down significantly India's mortality, disability, and injury rate during collisions. Let's doff our stylish helmets in anticipation of that.

CHAPTER 30

FROM START-UP TO SCALED-UP (2016)

There is no denying that India's e-commerce start-up "ecosystem" has come a long way. From a time when the only source of funding available to start-ups was the capital that passionate founders had to put together from friends and family, the situation has changed so dramatically that today funds chase ideas.

Indian start-ups have acquired valuations which make them bigger than manufacturing companies that have been listed on the Bombay Stock Exchange for decades. But a serious moment of self-reflection happened for this sector during the first half of 2016, besides dismaying tales of employees getting downsized or ventures going belly up.

And while there has been a fair amount of focus on the financial indicators by which start-ups need to be assessed post that moment, there has not been much talk about their current brand attributes versus desired brand attributes to make this a vibrant and vital sector of the economy.

Forget 'Funding'

The first brand attribute that needs to be recast is 'Funding.' In a gold-rush like mentality, many investors will put in money in half-baked ideas, hoping for an exit. Take the tiny example amongst many funded start-ups, of TinyOwl, the food-ordering app which got $16 million of Series B funding after an initial $4 million in Series A. Even an esteemed publication like Techcrunch announced this funding with the following additional information conveying TinyOwl's potential – "India's food ordering space is just one market booming in response to the growth of smartphones and mobile internet access in the county. An IDC report found India the fastest-growing smartphone market in Asia – over 23 million smartphones were shipped in Q3 2014, according to the firm, which represented an 82 percent growth on one year previously." We all know how the TinyOwl story ended.

This attribute of "Got Funding" where the amount of funding obtained defines the buzz around a start-up needs to be totally recast into the attribute of "sustained and scaled start-ups." The biggest brand attribute that needs to be built for the start-up ecosystem is to make an example of start-ups that have sustained and scaled over three or maybe five years. After all, the failure rate of start-ups is 90 percent, and if we add the factor of inability to scale, then that rate may go beyond 95 percent. India needs to know stories of start-ups that have not just sustained but also scaled significantly beyond three to five years by building a solid business. And it is these sustaining start-ups that need to be encouraged to go to campuses as they can not only provide a learning ground for freshers but also allow these freshers to channelise their change-the-world ideas.

Let's Drop 'Valuation'

The second brand attribute that needs to be recast is 'Valuation.' This "valuation" attribute needs to change into the attribute of "unique or well-adapted proposition." For decades, the cornerstone of success in India for global giants like Colgate, Palmolive, Unilever, Procter & Gamble and Cadbury's has been their ability to adapt their core propositions and make them relevant both in terms of product formulation and packaging. Think Sunsilk Sachets to Colgate Tooth Powder and the unique messaging adaptation of their core brand values. Who can forget the "*Kuch Khaas Hain*" campaign from Cadbury's, attempting to take chocolate consumption away from being just children-centric to young adults and doing it with a very Indian tone.

Now think of the adapted propositions in the e-commerce space. Most of them are just blind clones from other markets. If we look at the nine unicorns in India which have a valuation of $1 billion, then one realises that only Paytm, Inmobi, Zomato, Mu Sigma and Ola stand out in terms of "unique or well-adapted propositions."

Inmobi and Mu Sigma are absolutely unique in the mobile advertising and analytics space while Paytm has adapted the concept of digital wallets for Indian markets. Ola has done the same for cab hailing, and Zomato for restaurant listing and reviews. Others are mere clones of Amazon, ebay, Craigslist or many such global companies. That creates vulnerability for these unicorns, given India's distinct market dynamics and consumer preferences, but also provides a window for them to adapt and innovate.

Beware Discounts

The other attribute that has got associated with today's start-ups is 'Deep Discounting.' The only aspect that draws customers to these e-commerce sites is discounts. And when the funding dries up, the discounts disappear, the valuation plunges, and the vicious cycle of layoffs and closures begins.

The attribute that this needs to be converted into is 'Customer Experience.' Even if the start-up has a brilliant, game-changing idea, if the execution and linked customer experience do not match up, then the start-up will not sustain.

For all B2C e-commerce brands, the reference shifts to Amazon. But Amazon has been investing for years in never-before customer engagement algorithms to provide an unprecedented shopping experience at one end and in creating an incredible logistical infrastructure to deliver ahead of customer expectations at the other end.

Speaking to Amazon's physical growth, Jeff Bezos said in a rare interview that much of Amazon's profit goes directly back into development projects aimed to take Amazon even closer to its customers. Fulfilment centres geared around ultra-quick online-to-doorstep delivery and pick-up services are one such investment Bezos considers an important link between online and offline convenience.

Today, apps and sites in India claim food delivery in 30 minutes in India's crowded cities but except for putting pressure on a poor delivery boy on a bike, there is no clarity on what they are doing differently to support this claim.

Stories of such start-ups need to move away from this unsubstantiated claim and focus on whether they have done anything at all differently to deliver on such promises. Also, there is very little media focus on assessing the customer experience and satisfaction of e-commerce start-ups that have got lots of funding or have unprecedented valuations. From site experience to delivery to call centre to complaint handling, there are serious customer expectations that these start-ups need to deliver upon. Horror stories abound of unmet promises, wrong delivery of items, non-delivery and no shows and what not.

There needs to be a benchmark measure of customer experiences across all e-commerce start-ups that media covering the start-up sector needs to focus on. At present, media coverage is centred on making celebrities of start-up founders simply because they have secured $5 million of funding or achieved a valuation in someone's estimate of 500 million. There is nothing on the user experience and the service standards of these entities.

Start-ups that achieve these will not only continue to attract talent from India's top tier institutions but will never have to defer or rescind offers. And they will never be short of funding or valuations because the game-changing ideas and technologies from these freshers will always help them stay a step ahead of competition.

CHAPTER 31

THE AGE OF 'FLASH PHENOMENA'– WHY IS IT THAT SOME THINGS BECOME A GLOBAL RAGE AND THEN JUST DISAPPEAR? (2016)

Circle back to the end of 2012. If you stepped into a taxi in Dubai or even an auto rickshaw in Mumbai and asked the driver to switch on some music to make the journey lighter, there was a near 100 percent chance that the song that would get played, the words of which made no sense perhaps to anyone in Dubai or Delhi, was *Gangnam Style* by Psy.

Just imagine that a song largely in Korean about a lifestyle associated with a suburb in Seoul, laced with a catchy beat, and some amusing dance moves became a global phenomenon and topped music charts across thirty countries. Starting with some tweets by k-pop fans picked up by the social blog *Gawker*, then powered by comments or shares from celebrities such as Robbie Williams, Britney Spears and Tom Cruise, the song became a worldwide sensation, and then in a flash, disappeared.

People waited with huge anticipation for Psy's next release, *Gentleman*, but it never garnered the same kind of popularity as *Gangnam Style*. And while people remember that Gangnam phase, after a few months, the song simply disappeared from people's minds. It became what I call a 'flash phenomenon.' Just like how 'flash mobs' appear suddenly and then dissipate, we now live in an age of 'flash phenomena' in terms of media or even products, where some things become a global rage and then just disappear.

Think of the Christmas of 2009. The global financial crisis had just started. Cepia, a small company employing just sixteen people, released robotic hamsters as toy pets for children. These Zhu Zhu Pets, as they are called, became such a rage during the 2009 holiday season, that not only were many millions shipped, but the demand was so high that these $8 toys were selling for $60 on eBay. Perhaps it was the start of the recession that spurred customers to buy gifts which were just $8 in cost or maybe it was the insight that parents did not prefer real hamsters as pets and preferred these robotic versions. Whatever it was, Zhu Zhu Pets became the flash phenomenon of 2009. And while they still exist and have been extended into various other forms like video games, the craze for Zhu Zhu Pets peaked in the holiday-gifting season of 2009.

Should we say "Cow-u cow-u holy cow-u, I want u here now-u" to that? Because it brings me to the other flash phenomenon that seeped through our collective consciousness and became a part of our listening lives for a brief period of time – the 'Tanglish' song *Why this Kolaveri Di?* Nobody can quite explain the immense popularity for a brief period of time that resulted in this song getting more than 30 million views on YouTube, spreading across the world and becoming a rage even at, say, nightclubs in Japan. Even renowned publications such as *Time* magazine and respected international media such as BBC reported the popularity of this *Kolaveri* phenomenon. And then the craze disappeared. The movie that this song featured in came and went and did not even create a ripple.

This brings us to another product that became a rage and a must-have for some time, then declined and has now almost disappeared: The Nintendo Wii. Rather than competing against PlayStation and Xbox which were focused on creating hardware and software for serious gamers, Nintendo went for a strategy of making gaming fun and targeting casual as well as first-time gamers, and consumers who never had Xbox or PlayStation in their consideration sets. It paid off handsomely initially. The unique product with its Nunchuck controllers that appealed to even first-time gamers, and a marketing campaign that focused on different demographics, resulted in Wii being brought and enjoyed even by old people who had never considered playing video games ever during its peak.

Then by 2009, those very customers discovered another form of casual gaming and shifted. Touch-screen mobile phones and games such as Candy Crush and Farmville on Facebook are where the Wii customers started playing. The ongoing declines for Wii resulted in Nintendo actually discontinuing production of the Wii in most places such as Europe and Japan by 2013.

Realising the increasing penetration of smartphones, the fact that people are spending most of their time on smartphones and the GPS feature becoming a standard in almost all phones, Nintendo created another phenomenon in partnership with Niantic, the world's first augmented reality game Pokémon Go. Pokémon Go became such a rage that it eclipsed the likes of Candy Crush Saga and also started clocking revenues with its in-game purchases.

Besides the staggering numbers, marketers started trying to figure out how to get their brands associated with Pokémon Go. Restaurants and stores near Pokestops started offering discounts to players for gaining footfalls. Sports companies started exploring alliances as this was one game that actually made players active and forced them to be outdoors.

Many possibilities started emerging, especially in July 2016 when everything about the game peaked. But in three months, by end-September, the game had lost nearly 80 percent of its players. *Forbes* mentioned that the vaguely curious stopped playing. Pokémon Go now stands at the cusp of either sustaining the phenomenon it has unleashed or as ending up as just another flash phenomenon. Let's see what actually transpires.

And while I ruminate about the eventual fate of Pokémon Go and whether it will end up in the pantheon of the many flash phenomena, I receive a video on my Facebook account – "Pen Pineapple Apple Pen," goes DJ Piko Taro from Japan who has already been dubbed the next Psy. Inane but easy-to-remember lyrics, funny and easy-to-replicate dance moves, and a beat that keeps playing again and again in one's head. With more than 44 million views and counting, a new media flash phenomenon has struck again!

CHAPTER 32

SLOWING DOWN, GAINING RAPIDLY (2016)

We live our lives today in an always connected, ever-on world. At office, while going through some tough discussions, we simply open our Facebook application and get lost in checking what our friends are up to. On social occasions, when we want to switch off from banal conversations, we open our phones, pretend to be busy and start going through Whatsapp updates. During our morning walks, we'd rather not smell the flowers nor observe the potholes, but prefer to be blissfully lost in furiously keying in inane messages or having free conversations on Whatsapp.

Our food choices have also moved – not just to fast food, but our entire concept of lunch and dinner has changed. Modern always-on lifestyles now come with breakfast on the go, a working lunch on one's desk gobbled up quickly while staring at the computer screen or answering an email. And then comes dinner which is either eaten out or is something prepared by a cook early in the morning and microwaved. Some households even have cooks who come every four days or weekly and cook for an entire week.

But have you noticed something else that is happening? On always-on social media, there is a distinct pattern emerging of what people are sharing. Besides the usual jokes and happy anniversary pictures and the mandatory check-ins at first and business class lounges in airports all over the world, there are more and more shares on self-awareness, on self-improvement, on slowing down, on exercising more, on eating right, on desiring less, on calming ourselves and on meditating. As the extent of always-on connectivity keeps accelerating our already fast-paced existence, people increasingly across the world now desire to actually reflect, to disconnect, to find a purpose and to slow down.

Fast fashion has been a game-changer of our times, and brands such as Zara and H&M continue to grow rapidly. Providing seriously affordable styling for mass market consumers, the industry quickly puts new designs at economical prices, drawing back customers for repeat purchases. This concept of affordable and disposable fashion also brings with it challenges of pollution and of poor working conditions in underdeveloped countries. Now, as a counter to that there is an entire slow fashion movement both in terms of production and retail experience.

Take Officina Slowear from Italy. Contrary to the fast fashion approach, this brand mentions that 'the Slow' in its brand is because "slow" is everything that respects quality, workmanship, people and the environment – more than just a way of thinking about clothing, it is a whole lifestyle choice. The stores of this brand in different places, from Tokyo to Mexico City, do not look prefabricated but are designed to reflect that mood of that city. And the brand aims to create a home-like space to buy garments where one can pick up a book, listen to music and have a drink in the lounge area. A place to slow down, to touch and feel, not rush and buy.

The other issue is the polluting, sweatshop social challenge of disposable fashion. Now brands such as Patagonia have become mainstream with their focus on organic, recycled and environmentally-friendly fibres. Patagonia has emerged as a $750-million brand growing at 15 percent annually. There is a slew of slow fashion brands emerging and mainstreaming, ranging from Kowtow of New Zealand to funky, sustainability-focused brands such as Toad and Co.

As the fast food category continues to grow with even Indian cuisine restaurants moving to pre-cooked hub-and-spoke models, quick service restaurants, and extended franchises, there is a whole slow dining category also emerging. Slow Food International is a movement that encourages consumers to slow down and appreciate food once again, besides aiming to support local farmers and growers. The overall aim is to prepare and provide food that is good, clean and fair to everyone. Celebrity chef Jamie Oliver is one of the proponents of this slow food movement which aims to impart access to healthy and nutritious food to everyone while ensuring that food is created in an eco-sustainable way.

There is immense potential for mainstreaming this concept in India where it has only gathered selective acceptance with restaurants of the ITC Group and some establishments such as The Bohemian, Olive, The Bombay Canteen, and The Table or through Slow Food Farmers' Market events in Mumbai offering organic fresh fruits and vegetables from farmers across Maharashtra. At present, this phenomenon is restricted to premium restaurants and to organised events such as the market. In contrast, you walk around just the Central area in Hong Kong, and there are slow foods, organic, sustainable options such as Mana! offering fast slow food, Life Café and Eat Right. Slow and sustainable food options aplenty!

With eating out or ordering in becoming the norm in terms of eating habits across a rapidly-urbanising India, the idea of nutritious, freshly-cooked meals prepared from materials that help sustainability holds huge appeal. This is a branding phenomenon waiting to transition from niche, premium restaurants to mass outlets with affordable price points.

In today's fast-paced, interconnected world, the concept of slowing down and sustainability holds tremendous appeal across diverse categories from fashion to dining, with many global brands already realising the strength of this concept. It's time for marketers to revisit the *59th Street Bridge Song* from Simon and Garfunkel which said, "Slow down you move too fast, You got to make the morning last…" Embracing the 'slowing down' attribute may leave brands and their marketers "feelin' groovy."

CHAPTER 33

CMOS NEED TO GO TAKE A WALK (2017)

Thanks to a gracious Member of Parliament and a thorough gentleman like Sunil Dutt, we have been fortunate to have a jogger's park right in the middle of Lokhandwala Complex where my parents stay in Mumbai (India). And my favourite activity whenever I visit there is to go for a walk in the park with my dad. This has become a very special ritual for my dad and me, especially after our other partner, my mom, chose to go for a long walk in heaven last year. And, besides rich conversations and deep discussions, I have been observing the evolution of this park from a mere place to walk or run into a vibrant community. Some marketing possibilities have been realised and some areas yet untapped. After all, we are living our lives in an always-on world, lost in Whatsapp, Facebook, other social media or internet-related fixes, and totally lost from the real world. And it is at spaces like these parks where these ever-connected souls find time to breathe. While marketers are spending time sharpening their digital strategies to grab attention for their brands or categories on the internet, there is a whole new marketing possibility emerging where people converge as one community. And these are huge leverage opportunities for brands to tap into. Everyone who is paying a small fee and entering the park is doing so to burn some calories, get some endorphins and to get some fresh air. It is also a quieter and more receptive time as people are just walking or jogging and not lost in their phones or tablets. One fine day a cart turned up outside the park. From cucumber to aloe vera to tender coconut, this cart provides fresh and healthy beverages that people can drink to quench their workout-induced thirst and get some benefits. And slowly, a stop at the cart has become a matter of routine. Similar to that cutting chai stall near rickshaw stands or local train stations that people adopt into their commute. Just as a train journey to work should not start without that chai, the workout should end with one of these juices. Then afresh from the farm, the vegetable vendor showed up. Slowly, the fresh-mind-and-fresh-air seekers also started seeking fresh vegetables. Today, rows of expensive cars line up near the vendor after their morning strolls and jogs to get their daily straight from the farm supply of vegetables. Small billboards started coming up at the park – a great way to add an additional revenue stream for maintaining the park. But the brands present there are astrologers and realty companies. Clearly, some brand alignment is required here with the target audience and their attitudes. The fitness-and-freshness seeker is not out there seeking an astrologer. It seems straight out of the "*Sab Sach Karnewala Baba*" (quacks who promise a cure for all ills) posters in local trains. And if you need a personal trainer, then no need to look further. There are at least two or more available, offering different modes of training from learning how to jog despite a back problem, lessons to doing bicep-building, push ups and pull ups in the park lessons. While this marketing ecosystem has evolved, there is also considerable opportunity that lies untapped. The first obvious one is for brands like Adidas, Nike or Reebok. They can not only become brand sponsors of such parks but also provide on-site displays of their range from walking shoes for older folks to the appropriate running shoes for the middle-aged executive with a beer belly, training for his first half marathon due to peer pressure. Fitness equipment providers also have their audience right here. After all, what can the freshness seekers do when they cannot find the time to make it to the park? The portable exercising cycle at home can help. And what better place to get to know about this product then the park itself. Another huge opportunity is for furniture brands, specially chair-makers and back-support providers to sponsor or provide comfortable benches at the park. Besides the occasional giggly teenagers with raging hormones, most of the park benches are occupied by old people who need to sit after their walking quota or by exhausted runners trying to relax and recover. Comfortable chair-makers and other brands can provide a complete experience of their brand by substituting stone benches with their own products. Everyone walking into such parks is a wellness seeker of sorts. A psychographic segment for many of the wellness brands to tap into. From yoga and fitness centres to even pharmaceutical brands that promote general or alternate wellness like ayurveda and ayurvedic spas, etc., have a whole target audience waiting. For much of the crowds finishing their morning walks, there is also an opportunity for a periodical provider where people can buy their morning papers or evening tabloids. Additionally, a brand that no park user will ever forget is that benevolent brand which provides a tarpaulin cover to this park during the four plus months of the Mumbai monsoon when the park becomes wet or flooded and absolutely inaccessible. And while we all wait for that brand and park that thought physiotherapists and clinics can run campaigns during monsoon about their sprain, broken bones and hip treatment facilities for souls who still get to the flooded park despite the rain only to slip and fall. Given the number of actors and directors that frequent this park I am also waiting for some of the theatrically inclined to get together and stage their version of Neil Simon's plan – *Barefoot in the Park*. Now let me figure out during my next walk who looks a bit like Robert Redford and like Jane Fonda amongst the ever-increasing freshness seekers there.

CHAPTER 34

THE RISE OF D-BABAS! (2017)

I recently tried to connect with a close friend. Used the now almost-second-nature approach of getting in touch with pals whether they are in the same city or many continents away – I simply sent him a Whatsapp message. Knowing him as someone who responded to any Whatsapp within largely sixty minutes, I waited for his response and got none for almost 24 hours. I sent him another message. No response. When I finally called him to ask if he is ok, he promptly answered on the second ring. When I asked why he was not responding on Whatsapp, he said he is a D-Sanyasi or a D-Baba for 7 days. He has given up all things digital, especially phone and internet as a form of detox. While I have heard of people undertaking juice diets as a form of detox, or no alcohol phases to detox, I now realised that there is an increasing number of people who are choosing to get away from their always-on, always-connected devices, and trying periods of digital detox. And with the rise of the D-Babas comes news about the launch of products which are designed to appeal to digital seekers or help them in their quest for connecting with humans and not with devices. Think of the excitement that the relaunch of the Nokia 3310 by HMD Global has generated. Sure, there is truckloads of nostalgia associated with this phone from an entire generation that depended on this device for largely calling and texting. And there is the updated version of that game which is so playable that it becomes a passion – Snake – being relaunched. But more than all of that, the first point of excitement for the relaunched 3310 is that it has no internet connectivity. And it has that legendary nearly 30 days of standby battery life. Priced at just 50 euros, almost one-tenth the price of a basic iPhone, the Nokia 3310's relaunched version has been positioned as the ideal second phone to keep for those times when one wants to ditch technology and get back to the nostalgic and innocent days of calling and texting. And it became the biggest news to emerge at the Mobile World Congress held during March 2017 in Barcelona. Social media, press and the entire "connected" media went gaga over a non-internet-connection-based device at the most premier mobile technologies event in the world. No, it was not about Augmented Reality or Virtual Reality-linked phones or chatbots and what not, it was about a non-internet-enabled device that provided basic functionalities. This early buzz is a clear indicator of the rapidly emerging D-Sanyasi segment. Take another location which one assumes cannot exist without connectivity. When one enters a coffee shop today, behaviourally, one does not place an order first. One walks in and immediately asks for the WIFI password first and then decides on whether it is going to be a cappuccino or a latte. WIFI first, espresso later. So what will happen to people like us, if we land up at say Kibbitznest in Chicago which was covered in a very insightful article on the BBC website? It is a coffee shop which is also, hold your breath or rather your smart phone, a WIFI-free zone. Yes, there are no devices at this coffee shop nor is there any WIFI. People have their drinks and also have face-to-face conversations. And cafes such as this are springing up all over the US, London, Vancouver and beyond. The BBC article mentions that such coffee shops like Kibbitznest take us back to the reason why coffee shops existed – for debates, discussions and interactions. And to encourage more interactions, these coffee shops also have board games. A CNBC report in August 2016 mentioned that millions of Britons have been going on a digital detox. The article mentions a study undertaken by the British media and telecoms regulator Ofcom indicated that nearly a third of British internet users had gone on a digital detox at some time. A site called *It's time to log off* offers digital detox packages which aim to replace, in the site's own words, "endless mindless scrolling with mindful connection with nature and the great outdoors." Wired magazine in September 2016 also had a full article on trying a digital detox, likening it to a health food cleanse where one shuns screens just like one shuns bad food. It also mentions focusing on activities like knitting, baking or gardening to get away from that smart phone screen. Brands in these categories can really start focusing on the ever-growing tribe of digital detox seekers. There are so many opportunities for marketers to target this segment. But what about enforced digital detox? Well, I am certainly willing to pay a premium for cinema halls that ban smart phone browsing when the movie is on. At present, the movie experience in India's famed multiplexes is to buy a 25 USD ticket, settle in your seat and then watch five or six smart phones glowing brighter than the movie screen in the seats ahead, with movie watchers more interested in Whatsapping, tweeting and Facebooking than watching the movie. If only cinema halls would become mandatory digital detox centres for three hours. And if some of the cinegoers refuse to become D-Babas even for three hours, then they might as well watch ads for three hours from R-Baba's Patanjali brand rather than watching a full movie.

CHAPTER 35

THE NEED FOR SENIOR CITIZENS' BANKS (2017)

A bank customer gets a call from an overzealous telecaller during their afternoon nap, offering a credit card. An erroneously mentioned 'yes' results in a card, a statement, fees, late payment charges and a bad credit history. Now imagine if that customer is a septuagenarian widower living by himself. This is a recurring grim reality of today's sales-focused, outsourcing-dependent banking sector.

India is a 'young' country. But there is a different dimension to this 'young demographic' attribute. Census indicates more than 104 million people are aged 60 years and above – a segment likely to go up to 300 million by 2050. This is a demographic that is almost the size of entire countries such as Vietnam or Egypt. And they are living by themselves due to changing social structures.

Banking propositions for this segment do not extend beyond slightly higher rates on deposits with some insurance covers and free-for-life debit cards. Banks just assume all their customers are internet, smartphone and debit/credit product savvy. They often ignore the septuagenarians, octogenarians, and nonagenarians – "The Passbook Generation" – who are more comfortable with old-world pass books, cheque books and branch visits.

Banking propositions for this segment need to evolve and consider:

1) Home delivery: Even diagnostic centres now come home. Banks can provide a similar home delivery service for services such as delivering cash, collecting cheques, premiums, repayments and updating passbooks.

2) Special services: Akin to services for high-worth individuals, banks can provide allocated parking space, wheel chairs, designated areas in the branch for transactional needs and even dedicated relationship managers.

3) Healthcare cover: To solve the challenge of inadequate medical cover, bank accounts can provide free medical insurance plus discounted medical cover options to senior citizens. The coverage scope should include dental and optical care besides travel insurance options.

4) Faster clearance: This segment heavily relies on pension funds or remittances from their children. Preferred exchange rates, instant credit and a simple call from the bank can make a significant difference.

5) Bill management: This segment cannot wait in queues, and if net savvy, they are prone to keying in wrong account numbers or card numbers. Now imagine if the bank-at-home service includes collecting and paying all due bills.

6) Money management: Old people have regular assessable incomes coming through pensions, rent or interests. They aspire to travel or need cars with drivers, given the difficulty of commuting in our cities. Banks need to structure segment-specific auto, travel and home refurbishment loans. Besides preferred rates, such loans can come with value-added benefits such as discounts on services that provide drivers and offers from travel agents.

7) Value-added benefits: Banks can also provide value-added benefits to this community for enhancing their fitness, like discounted and exclusive time slots at gyms and fitness centres.

CHAPTER 36

FROM COST-FIRST TO CUSTOMER-FIRST (2017)

Recently, State Bank of India announced service charges for accounts that do not meet balance qualifiers and also announced charges for cash withdrawal and cash deposits based on defined thresholds. Just yesterday, SBI revised charges once again on a host of services. Private banks already have similar charging structures, and these entire set of charges merit questioning on a number of fronts.

Technology: The cost of technology-linked infrastructure and of connectivity continues to come down. For e.g., cellphone charges with internet are lower now than the cost of STD calls some years ago. Banks are using the same technology platforms, so why should the cost to the customer actually go up at this stage when all linked infrastructural costs continue to decline?

Cost rationalisation: Banks have been investing heavily in minimising cost to serve. From centralising operations to outsourcing to focusing on mobile and digital, banks are going all out to reduce cost to serve. So, why would charges need to increase again at this juncture? Networked ATMs are becoming the norm. And vibrant organisations like the National Payments Corporation of India continue to reduce switching charges on Rupay transactions for ATMs as well as bringing down merchant discount rates to drive PoS transactions. These benefits need to flow to customers.

Lower interest rate on deposits: Banks have to pay interest on saving accounts and on fixed deposits. But both of these rates have only been going one way – down. Incidentally, the lowest rate on deposits is offered by SBI – 6.5 percent for three- and five-year tenures. So why should service charges increase at this juncture?

Current accounts: Service charges for current accounts have also been revised. This is a surprise because banks provide no interest rates on current accounts. And even if a bank is providing 4 percent interest rate on a savings account, it can lend at the lowest level in the interbank market at 6–7 percent with a 2-percent margin to make a revenue of Rs. 300 annually on an account with an average balance of Rs. 15,000, which is classified as below the qualifier of Rs. 25,000 minimum average daily balance.

Finally, such a step can be attributed to the banking sector's overall drive to ramp up fee income which is risk-free and hence valued in a high-NPA environment. However, the same can be achieved in different ways without simply increasing or adding charges. For example, debit card usage at PoS machines instead of for cash advances can be promoted by providing relevant loyalty programmes such as reward points, miles or cash back.

Similar incentives can be offered for internet banking enrolment and usage. Also, overdraft facilities can be embedded with debit cards to create an additional revenue stream for banks and to protect customers when they run out of balance. And, any fees and charges can be linked to value-added insurance features in areas such as card protection, credit protection on overdrafts, protection against fraudulent transactions, etc.

This will also benefit the insurance industry and help drive insurance penetration amongst underpenetrated segments defined as those that cannot meet the qualifying balance criteria of banks.

Overall, the perspective has to move from cost-plus to customer-plus and customer-first.

CHAPTER 37

REBOOTING THE "CURRY" CATEGORY (2017)

Imagine a situation where there is not just demand but an inherent craving for a category. And this craving spans across a market of not just one or two million people but a potential forty to fifty million people. And this is a category that is growing by at least ten percent a year. Too good to be true. Well actually true, real and surprisingly; it is truly, deeply and madly underserved. Look at any statistic, and it indicates that 16 million Indians live outside India and another 20 million plus travel abroad every year. Both these numbers keep growing every year. And the one thing that Indians crave on long trips abroad or when they are staying in remote corners of the world, adding to India's remittance flow, is Indian food. Classy Indian restaurants are springing up and providing never-before experiences in premium dining. These are a class apart but not for everyone –business class and first class equivalents. In terms of regular dining, let us look at the staple offering in this category. The standard experience amounts to something straight out of that Aasif Mandvi movie *Today's Special*. After searching for an Indian restaurant and excited at the thought of good old "dal chawal and some parathas," you make your way to the place. Amidst a row of other fancy-looking restaurants, you see a dimly-lit outfit with a good chance of any of these three words appearing as a prefix or a suffix – 'Tandoori' or 'Namaste' or 'India.' Inside the dimly-lit interiors, you find upholstery which was used by another restaurant for twenty years and then passed on here and has been in use for another five years. A trademark musty or damp odour also emanates. Unwashed dishes of the last patrons lie in tubs all around. Perhaps there is even that spitting cook of *Today's Special* lurking inside. A look at the menu makes the entire AIDA concept melt into one; Awareness, Interest, Desire all Awakened and that too at once. Ravenously, orders are placed, and then the food arrives. Ahem. The standard experience can be summarised into three broad attributes – Grime, Grease and Gluten. Grime – the overall upkeep reeks of cut corners everywhere. Grease – as if Indian food is only about grease and more grease. Gluten – and that too the refined flour variety served in full excess. Most places also have a policy of "going green," but with a covenant. There is recycling but only of used oil. After all, the more oil is reused, the better it makes the food taste. Then comes the bill. Largely, the bill in foreign currency is comparable to the price of a near-premium restaurant. And finally, the memento. Like a voter's mark, the red or green colour additives in the gravy leave green or red marks that no hand soap brand has provided a solution for removal. It takes at least ten plus washes and many days to fade, and by then many people will know that you have just paid a visit to Grease Palace. Yes, there are super premium and world class Indian restaurants all over the world, but the standard fare is pretty much as above. And with demand far outstripping supply, there is a huge opportunity to reboot this category in so many ways – shift from curry in a hurry, laced with *papadums*, into fresh food prepared with fresh ingredients and periodically refreshed menus; pleasing décor – bright, clean and functional; greased chairs not greased food; and food that moves from just "tastes good" to "tastes good and does good." After all, getting quality chefs to move to different parts of the world is not a challenge at all. And a 40 million plus potential awaits – in addition to the millions of non-Indians who enjoy Indian cuisine now – and will frequent a fresh, clean, non-greasy food place. Till then all we can do is hope that Saravana Bhawan – the gold standard in terms of Indian food – has already expanded its footprint and opened an outlet wherever we are planning to travel or move out of India. Standardised and hygienic, they have perfected the formula for getting it right anywhere in the world.